For my daughters: Rachel and Rebekah

CONTENTS

PREFACE

~~~~~~~~~~

T HIS BOOK is intended for students who need to write well to get into college. It offers in a brief space a complete course in the elements of composition needed for students to present themselves with clear-edged precision to an application committee. It covers the essentials of writing, by which I mean the methods by which a writer can use good seeing, feeling, and thinking to represent himself or herself in three dimensions in prose. For college admissions, this almost always means writing in the first person about things from the world of a writer's own experience. It also means beginning to find an orderliness in that experience that lends itself to vivid expression in narrative. But good narratives do not come out of nowhere. They have to be found, and the various means by which good narratives can be found, developed, and extended are the subject of this book.

A college application is first and foremost a narrative about the person writing it. Students can often recognize good narratives when they read them, but they are often weak in understanding their component parts. Much of this book is taken up with explaining how good narratives fit together and how the unity of narrative can also be used to unify a college application. Understanding how good narratives fit together means studying examples in detail, which I do. Narratives have an integrated voice. Students are often encouraged to find their own voice, but they are only infrequently told how hard it is to find it on their own. The great English painter Sir Joshua Reynolds once said, "the more extensive your acquaintance is of the works of those who have excelled, the more extensive will be your powers of *invention*." An inventive college essay does not come out of a vacuum but is the carefully constructed result of choices a writer has made, one by one. This quality of self-awareness in self-expression is one of the things colleges are looking for in applicants. It involves knowing what one is saying and understanding where what one is saying comes from.

A strong application also involves a sense of overall design. Most college applications do not fit together very well. Many students want to put as much information as possible about themselves in their applications, but much of what they set down seems closed off from who they actually are. They are full of common outer experiences whose inner meaning the writer seems to regard as self-evident. And they are full of common ambitions whose ends and aims the writer seems to regard as self-justifying. As writers, many students have not yet learned to attach words to experience with any accuracy of import or meaning. The result is an application that often reads like a series of questions to answers on a test. There is simply no sense of a unified person behind the words. It then becomes perilously easy for a reader to see the writer as nothing more than a series of glimpses and anecdotes. In everyday life, we constantly piece together images of people from limited evidence. But in a college application, such a fragmentary treatment has a very good chance of being rejected.

Many people try to teach students how to write admissions essays. This book teaches students how to write by writing the admissions essay. This is not a general handbook of rules for composition but a method for composing one particular kind of essay. I try at every point to give students the power of choice over how to represent themselves. Most admissions essays rely on standard forms of self-representation played out in preformed, widely shared narratives. I have tried to work out a method to free students from the crushing regularity of these narratives, discovering a means of expression that comes closest to how they actually see themselves. Writing well means being open to their own experience, whatever it is, their sense impressions, their memories, and their feelings about them, and all the learning they have come to carry around with them after years of schooling. Writing well also means being open to the experience of studying great writings, selected to show them the beginnings of a way forward. The resulting essay comes as close as possible to being a trustworthy representation of a whole person at a moment in time.

But not just at a moment in time. Many college application essays present frozen selves and do not account for all the pulls and forces that make a person complex. Here is where, coming to this work, I felt I had a special training. I am a novelist and literary critic. I have spent my life trying to understand why some representations of life and character are vivid, while others are wanting. Novels and short stories show the development of character over time, responding to the pressure of events. They can be studied in and of themselves, but they can also be used as models for how to present character in a rounded way. In *Aspects of the Novel*, E. M. Forster speaks of flat and round characters. A flat character is one who is "easily recognized whenever they come in." This is because "they are constructed around a single idea or quality." A round character is one who is multidimensional. Most admissions essays suffer from the problems of flat characters in fiction. They never develop. But they suffer from another problem as well. In fiction, flat characters rarely pose as round characters. In most admissions essays, a flat character is being presented as round, usually because the writer is unaware of the means by which a rounded character is created in prose. The flatness can have many sources. There can be a flatness in language, but there can also be a flatness in observation, emotion, or thought. I will cover these forms of flatness in detail later. What matters here is that, as Forster says, except for one governing impulse, the flat character "has no existence outside it." In an admissions essay, this limiting impulse may be a typical ambition (becoming a doctor or lawyer) or a common activity (belonging to a team or an organization). They are easily remembered, but for all the wrong reasons, for they are never changed by circumstances and are often close to caricature.

A round character is much harder to create. A round character, says Forster, "cannot be summed up in a single phrase." More than this: "the test of a round character is whether it is capable of surprising in a convincing way." This is because round characters act unexpectedly. They experience life directly and change in response to it. They face contradictions and incongruities and have to work their way through them, often with no clear end in mind. A certain sense of process always exists around them. Think of Pip in Charles Dickens's *Great Expectations*. He is always changing, growing, half in the dark and half in the light, passing through a world of odd angles, strange characters, and small details whose meaning is by no means always clear to him. The more he sees, the more he changes, and the more his self-conscious awareness advances and matures. This maturity comes as he finds solid points of reference in his life and comes to experience it as it is, not in terms of some remote past or imagined future. As the novel proceeds, he struggles to reconstrue some very basic aspects of his experience, and by its end he sees the girl he loves, Estella, and the convict who assists him, Abel Magwitch, very differently than he does at the beginning. His life is an object lesson in changeability, and the novel that tells his story is a beautiful example of a fully integrated voice narrated in the first person.

Crafting an integrated voice is the basic work of the admissions essay. A voice that is round, not flat, because it speaks from a unity of seeing, feeling, and thinking. A good application has the quiet unity of an integrated personality. Like a rounded character, it leaves us with the dominant impression of having lived for a time with someone we seem to know well. Given its shortness, an application essay is actually a kind of portrait in miniature, but it is a miniature that is never two-dimensional. The essay may begin by trying to answer a formulaic question from a prompt (*Discuss an Accomplishment, Describe an Interest*), but it gradually moves away from the formula into a space where the formula no longer pertains. Jane Austen once described her writing as "the little bit of ivory (two inches wide) on which I work with so fine a brush." She was being modest, of course, but in talking about the work I do with students, I am often asked how it is possible to do anything at all within the very small frame of an admissions essay. I have written this book to show how it is possible, even in the scope of one or two pages, to use the craft of writing to give weight and force to words.

ACKNOWLEDGMENTS

My thanks go out to those people who have helped me imagine and then write this book. They are Danny Harrington, Sue Smith, Michael Li, Donald Ross, Markus Hoffmann, and Greg Britton. My students over the past ten years also deserve thanks, for it is through them that I have come to the method of this book. My greatest thanks go to my wife, Elizabeth Kleber, and to our daughters, Rachel and Rebekah, who always have made me mindful of placing everything I say in a clear and understandable context.

ADMIT ONE

Introduction

THIS BOOK is a different kind of guide to college admissions. It considers how you can present yourself for evaluation without being reliant on the evaluations of others. It lays out a way for you to understand grades and test scores for what they are—thin, sketchy accounts that are by no means authoritative. And it shows you how you can begin to find an order in your own experience, which, when communicated in good prose, will allow you to shape your own perceptions so that there can be a resonance in them for others.

Applying to college does not have to be in any way artificial, a matter of mere self-presentation before a committee. I have been tutoring high school students for over ten years, and during that time, I have found again and again that preparing a college application

1

can, in fact, be a means of self-discovery, and the further students progress in developing their own inward integration (an integration I see specifically as an integration of voice), the more likely they are to be seen as fellow pilgrims by the best schools in the country and get in.

～～～～～～～～

There are no secrets to getting in, but there is an art. A good application forms a single narrative, and the different parts of the application—essay, supplements, letters, and transcript—should all contribute to it.

This narrative can best be understood as a hybrid of fiction and nonfiction. Using many of the techniques of fiction, which give it an immediacy of feeling and expression, it tells a story—your story, or more likely, just a small part of it—but it also shows an openness to the meaning of that story. Even more, it explicitly owns that meaning and is interpretative and often introspective. Though suggestive and short, it nevertheless shows a movement toward an integration of thought. The schools themselves are looking for an incipient intellectual maturity, an open awareness of ideas and their shaping power. In this sense, simply telling your own story in an application is not enough. The great universities see themselves as places for disturbing the universe. They are looking for people whose locus of evaluation exists primarily within themselves, people who do not necessarily look to others for approval or disapproval. A good application will give the person evaluating it the feeling of looking in on a very interesting life, a self-chosen life undertaken for its own sake. It does not need to be a complete life or a fully realized one. But there has to be a specific intellectual tilt to what you are saying about yourself. That is where how you write matters. You have to learn to write about yourself in a way that invests ideas with feeling and feeling with ideas. You have to find a voice. This is hard for even the best writers to do. It comes out of hard-won self-knowledge.

Here, it is worth remembering that our American system of admissions gives students a real opportunity for self-representation. In this, it is unique among admissions systems found elsewhere in the world, where numbers often trump words. There is something deeply democratic about allowing every applicant the potential of an integrated voice. Note that I say "potential." Very few writers ever find a truly distinctive voice, and fewer still find it when young. But it is my experience that in trying to find a voice, writers become more and more themselves. They first begin by dropping the facades that front the shared streets of life. Then in language they find, for the first time, not a system of rules, but a set of possibilities to be experienced all the way to their limit. Language, openly experienced, opens writers to all that the senses report. Writers have said over and over again that in writing, they find unknown parts of themselves and also, conversely, become more aware of the world as it exists outside of themselves.

Writing allows you to let your own experience tell you its own meaning, to discern tendencies in yourself, tendencies that, in time, become autonomous and mature into real and solid directions. It involves being open to your own private perceptual world and allowing it to enrich the choices you make as you prepare for college. It also allows you to take risks within your own frame of reference, to experiment with your own thoughts and feelings, and to be changed by them. You learn to make a place for your inner world in your outer world.

~~~~~~~~~~

Strange as it may seem, the hardest part of this is learning to permit yourself to do it. I found this out for myself. I learned what I thought a college application should look like by helping students try to find their way toward one. The way was not at all clear at first. Students came to me because they were having trouble with their applications. In some cases, it was a matter of numbers. Their scores or grades were low. But in many cases, it was a matter of understanding. Faced with very steep odds—one in ten, or even worse—they no longer knew what to do. They had done everything they were told to do, and yet it was clear that it was no longer enough. They had no idea how to act constructively toward a clear end. Coming into my office, their emphasis was often on weaknesses rather than strengths. They thought I might know how to add a few more points to their scores or grades. The writing of the essay barely registered with them. To the extent it figured at all in their thoughts, it was like a coloring book where they were being told to fill in an existing picture with a box of crayons. Over and over again I found out just how little of themselves they saw in the applications they were completing. The procedure seemed to demand a certain fixity, and they responded in kind.

By fixity, I do not mean a fixed number but a fixed way of being. Very few of my students seemed to value any part of college admissions as a learning experience. Though long and difficult, it lacked any sense of educational *process*. The application itself often appeared to them as a series of carefully constructed pigeonholes. There was no fluidity to the experience of compiling it. Preparing to apply, there was very little to the moment of *now* except for a vague sense that this miserable moment would pass once they met the deadline. Preparing the application was essentially a long stretch of dead time doing what *had* to be done in the most efficient way possible. The idea of prolonging the process did not in any way appeal to them. I was there solely to speed it up and help them feed it into the machine, which in this case, was a real machine, the Common Application. Many suspected they were only putting together very simplified pictures of themselves. Many also suspected that these pictures they were putting together of themselves for schools to see were significantly at variance with the pictures of themselves that they carried around, but they simply felt that, from where they stood, there was nothing they could do about it.

I started to see how fraught the entire experience was. Parents and students face two realities. The first is what they are being told to do by high schools and college admissions offices. Initially, it can seem like common sense. Follow the rules as though nothing has changed. Take the tests, get the grades, volunteer for everything. The second reality does not take long for them to uncover. Schools where the chance of admission is one in twenty. Tests that can be gamed. Tutors in every discipline. Résumés that have to be packed. Counselors who barely know them, yet steer them into schools that are "right" for them. And the fear that other students and parents may well be one step ahead of them in gaming the system. To many, it feels like there is scarcely any kind of order left in it. They begin the process with a faith that someone, somewhere, is measuring something and end it with a sense that no form of measurement, anywhere, is working. Students see so little of themselves in the means directed at evaluating them that it causes them to distrust their own experience. The fact that the whole process is self-limiting, and, in many instances, relatively brief, makes it all the harder to evaluate the experience. After a few months most students have received their acceptances and rejections and most would prefer just to move on. They can hardly be blamed for trying to accept what has happened to them. It gives a bad double meaning to the term "acceptance."

I knew I had to find a new way of being for the college application, so I came to it as a writer. I thought that, being partly written, it at least had some possibilities for self-expression in narrative. By narrative I mean the broadest sense of the creative use of language. I'd often had the thought that the basic tools of the testing trade—the multiple choice questions, the passages taken out of context, and the deceitful vocabulary—manage inadvertently to bring together the ugliest things about language by ransacking it for little tricks of logic and organization. But what, I thought, if the process could be made beautiful? What if students could come to see writing not as some kind of arcane special capacity but as a core expression of who they were? What if the completed application could read like a good story, full of sharply observed things united in a single voice? What if it could not just speak but *sing*?

It took me a number of years to clear the ground for a new approach. I made many mistakes in looking for a new form of expression in the college application before I began to find my way. The order in which I came to these ideas is by no means the same as the order in which I have chosen to present them here. In this book, I have tried to take from my process of working with students the simplest ideas best able to describe it. These go to seeing, feeling, and thinking as the basis for finding an authentic voice in writing. In chapters on voice, words, sentences, and paragraphs, I have tried to present an orderly way of thinking about writing as building on perception, emotion, and thought. I see writing as most powerful when it establishes a high degree of congruence between the three. I started working with students on the personal essay because that essay seemed to have a good chance of having just those elements of seeing, feeling, and thinking that make for great writing. Young people see things with freshness and feel them with force, and if they are taught stepwise to come to thought based firmly on what they see and feel, rather than relying on the thoughts of others or the fixed forms of organization taught in handbooks, they can write with great clarity and power and effectiveness. The result is not expository but exploratory, an exercise in grounded and focused self-exploration. Simply by trying to write their thoughts down they become aware of many thoughts of which they were previously unaware, and they can get better at it as they go along, in ways that can be clearly demonstrated to them. The personal essay will never be a fully intellectual document like a college paper, but it can show a life taking on an intellectual tilt as a private perceptual world searches for a more public expression. The resulting essay is what allows the admissions committee to see past the numbers to the student.

I have also found it is possible to translate this understanding of the central position of writing into a new way of looking at the application as a whole. This I call "the narrative-based application." Its major tenets have been largely implicit in what I have been doing for many years. It involves a simple act of reorientation that has large consequences. I ask my students to think of their application as a single narrative, as something like a small novella of their life, a master narrative told in different parts. To this end, I have my students tell small, striking stories about themselves, studying, for example, how Ernest Hemingway does it in *In Our Time* or how Sandra Cisneros does it in *The House on Mango Street*. Then they can treat the supplemental questions essentially as a short story sequence but in a very quiet way. They learn to build up a picture made of many small parts that come together as a whole. A narrative application allows the sense of a finely tuned understanding of a complete person to be conveyed to others. And not only to them. Once accepted, wherever they are accepted, my students say they feel known and confirmed. One of the saddest things to hear any student say is that someone must have made a mistake in letting them in. Among my students I have seen this sense of *not* belonging largely vanish because, having represented themselves well, they feel their acceptance as confirmation rather than chance. Getting in, they feel *seen*, valued in their very identity, and ready to proceed. The experience of rejection changes as well, for less and less do my students look for admission to one particular school. My students know that, whatever the result, they have succeeded in representing themselves to others at the far reach of their own development. As *writers* they have found things in themselves that, often, they did not know were there and are often in a state of wonder that such exciting new directions have come out of them.

In this book, I draw together this sense of writing as central to admissions into a more coherent picture. The book lays out a complete process of writing an admissions essay from the ground up. It shows what to do and what not to do, going over the use of words, sentences, and paragraphs. It follows one so-so essay getting better and better with many intervening changes. And more, it advises students on how to use their writing as the leading edge of their intellectual development. I try to do this in plain language, using terms that any high school student can grasp. People vary in how they learn, but in my experience, students very much enjoy improving their ability to tell their own stories. They readily see that the techniques I show them, by making them more effective as storytellers, make them more memorable as applicants. I also think they see it as genuinely intellectual work. Time spent studying for standard tests dead-ends with the tests, and nearly everyone hates the experience from beginning to end. But time spent learning how to write actually prepares students for college. Writing well will not take the stress out of applying to college. But it does make the act of applying more mindful and the results more trustworthy.

I

~~~

Voice

MOST COLLEGE applications suffer from a discrepancy of voice. That is, there is a complete division between the writer's own experience and how it is expressed. The words on the page are there, but they do not seem to have anything behind them. The words feel cut loose from feeling, even though they purport to express it. They also feel devoid of thought, even though, at times, they lurch toward it. The writing can actually seem writerless.

This is because the words on the page do not seem so much actively chosen, taken in, as passively received. The words are often clear but are somehow peripheral to the reality being described. This can be true even when an immediate setting is clear and the writer's attitude toward it can be discerned.

If the very idea of this division of voice seems strange, let me try to show it in action. It takes a certain adjustment of one's sights to begin to perceive it. It helps to see examples. Here are the first three paragraphs from one student's personal essay:

I visited a mine last year in West Virginia. It was part of a consciousness-raising trip with the Student Environmental Alliance. Not that we could get in. The corporation running the mine made sure to keep us outside the gate. They only opened the gates when the miners came out. They looked tired. We tried to give them brochures about how coal was contributing to global warming but they did not seem too interested. Then the corporation sent someone out to talk to us. We debated whether to listen to him but decided by consensus that his view already dominated the media and that he perpetuated the problem through his inaction. Instead we presented him with our demands, which included making a firm and immediate commitment to decreasing global consumption of fossil fuels.

On the way back we sang old protest songs on the bus. It was very poignant. We talked about keeping close to nature's heart, and also about larger systemic issues and the need to dismantle institutions that promote global warming. First and foremost was the need to structurally address issues central to the well-being of the workers in the industry. My contribution was the idea of the Transformation Budget. The companies would set up a fund to reeducate their workers to participate in globally solvent technologies such as wind power and solar cells or other ecologically non-harmful careers. Or maybe geothermal, because that may just be the wave of the future. I told my classmates we had to do something soon, because we won't have a society left if we destroy the environment.

A vision of social justice led to the civil rights move-ment a generation ago. A vision of global environmental justice is what is bringing me to college now. I want to take a thought-leadership role in making the world a better place for all its citizens. My plan is to major in a field that challenges social injustice or to create one of my own. I sometimes call this "oppression studies." If those miners I saw knew about the erasure and reconstruction of history that has led to the massive overconsumption of coal, I feel certain that they would have joined us that day on the barricades in West Virginia.

Thousands of college essays sound just like this one. They have a public quality and an easy journalistic flow, even though the actual experience described, vis-iting a mine, seems rather remote here except for the passing statement, never examined, that the miners "looked tired." The ideas are few and clear. Coal min-ing is condemned unequivocally. No benefits are seen in the human use of coal. A certain rigid self-righteous-ness pervades the tone. Certainly there is an underly-ing anger in it, the anger of the writer at a world that is slow to change. But the narration lacks a complete experiencing of the events it narrates. It could easily be skimmed and would not long be remembered. Though it has clarity, it lacks voice.

It is important to ask why.

Weak writing is often so cloudy that it is hard to get at its underlying presuppositions. They are so often not there or just barely there. Look more closely at the passage. Many statements in it feel as though they have come from somewhere else. In fact, they have. "Keeping close to nature's heart" is from John Muir. "Not having a society left if we destroy the land" is a reformulation of Margaret Mead. Many of the other statements lack basic agency. Who, after all, does the erasing of history? Who, exactly, are the judges that will sit on the court that brings about "global environmental justice"? Others are simply bad old clichés, such as "barricades," that staple of revolutionary jargon from the Paris Commune. A few lines even sound like advertising, though in saying geothermal "may just be the wave of the future," the writer appears tone-deaf to the menace embedded in the idea of a mighty sweeping wave. That each of these undigested sentences distantly represents a cry of feeling in the author is undeniable, though the writer's one explicit effort in that direction, "poignant," far from evoking emotion, verges on the sentimental. The cry is hidden behind a commonness of statement.

The passage is easy to read but for all the wrong reasons. Whatever is being said, we have the feeling we have heard it all before. Reading here is reduced from a challenge to a confirmation. And this feeling we have is compounded by a suspicion that the writer has little awareness of being so far removed from the origin of the many statements made. Not one word in the passage feels as though it has any direct reference to the life, as lived, of the writer or the miners seen in passing. The words chosen tend to freeze and narrow perception, and the writer seems to have no clear idea of what needs to be moved away from, except for that one word, coal. Note, too, how little surprise there is in this text. There is no desire to register external events internally or even to learn anything the writer does not already know. The experience described throughout is that of the writer being in complete agreement with a small group of like-minded people. There is no sense of dialogue, and the one opportunity for it, with the corporate spokesman, is, tellingly, refused. Indeed, the troubling substratum of the piece is the utter unanimity of the protesters, who want to go from not being in charge to being in charge. The writer's one neologism, a "thought-leadership role," is almost Orwellian. It implies a leader, or a cadre of them, who leads by imposing thoughts on others. There are no private worlds here, not even the quiet suffering of the miners themselves, and no discernibly individual people. There is only a clash of public worlds in which one large force, representing a kind of good, replaces another, representing a kind of evil. It is a distinctly immature vision of life in which a young writer con-founds conviction with truth.

There is a painful aspect to reading a well-inten-tioned essay like this. The writers are often so much less than what they are presenting themselves to be. A person is never wholly a figment of writing, of course, but a passage such as this actually impedes rather than advances a reader's knowledge of a writer. The truth is that it is very difficult to know a person from bad writing, especially when a writer wants to be heard without listening to himself or herself. The person is not physically present to allow us to make small corrective adjustments. The best we can do from the foregoing passage is to make a tentative hypothesis that the writer, having heard things from various sources, has become interested in social justice. No specific academic direction is clear. An admissions committee reading such an essay would be thrown back to the evidence of grades, scores, and letters. In this case, the unintended consequence of this personal essay would be to make the act of admission highly impersonal and much less likely as a result. It is a reminder that these essays can backfire. It may well be that the writer is only trying on ideas for size, and that these one-size-fits-all concepts will not wear well over time. Only time will tell, but admissions committees do not have it.

~~~~~~~~~~

Listen, now, to George Orwell in *The Road to Wigan Pier*, who describes visiting a mine and starting to think quietly about what he had seen when he saw some miners coming out of it:

When the miner comes up from the pit his face is so pale that it is noticeable even through the mask of coal-dust.

This is due to the foul air that he has been breathing, and will wear off presently. To a Southerner, new to the mining districts, the spectacle of a shift of several hundred miners streaming out of the pit is strange and slightly sinister. Their exhausted faces, with the grime clinging in all the hollows, have a fierce, wild look. At other times, when their faces are clean, there is not much to distinguish them from the rest of the population. They have a very upright square-shouldered walk, a reaction from the constant bending underground, but most of them are shortish men and their thick ill-fitting clothes hide the splendour of their bodies. The most definitely distinctive thing about them is the blue scars on their noses. Every miner has blue scars on his nose and forehead, and will carry them to his death. The coal dust of which the air underground is full enters every cut, and then the skin grows over it and forms a blue stain like tattooing, which in fact, it is. Some of the older men have their foreheads veined like Roquefort cheeses from this cause.

Reality has a refractory hardness here. The world may not be what Orwell wishes it to be, but the fact of it can be felt and touched. The miners have blue scars on their noses! Orwell is not trying to see more than what he sees and is not racing to come to a conclusion about it. As a result, his mind is free to move in any direction. Here is what he comes to:

Watching coal-miners at work, you realise momentarily what different universes people inhabit. Down there where coal is dug is a sort of world apart which one can quite easily go through life without ever hearing about. Probably a majority of people would even prefer not to hear about it. Yet it is the absolutely necessary counterpart of our world above. Practically everything we do, from eating an ice to crossing the Atlantic, and from baking a loaf of bread to writing a novel, involves the use of coal, directly or indirectly. For all the arts of peace coal is needed; if war breaks out it is needed all the more. In time of revolution the miner must go on working or the revolution must stop, for revolution as much as reaction needs coal. Whatever may be happening on the surface, the hacking and shoveling have got to continue without a pause, or at any rate without pausing for more than a few weeks at the most.

There are ideas here, but without any tilt of bias. Even more, Orwell manages to preserve a sense of wonder that such a state of affairs could ever come into being. This wonder allows him to probe his world with ever-increasing perceptual acuity. Reading Orwell is like seeing a distant object come into focus through the lens of a telescope. But with one crucial difference: his vision is never cold. Orwell combines a sharpness of vision with a warmth of empathetic understanding. He searches not for the outlines of answers but for the basic dimensions of a problem. He can often see some strange things in the process, too, such as the miners' blue scars. Note too that he rarely asks the question, "What does it mean?" This would push the problem too far away from the world with a single stroke. Rather, his habitual question is, "What is going on here?" Having asked it, he is there with us to sort out the implications, which are often surprising. It may well be that the one thing a reader remembers, years later, about *The Road to Wigan Pier* is not the conditions in the mines but the blue scars on the noses of the miners who work in them. In doing so, he excellently catches a quandary in which society finds itself without offering a set of fixed views about it. Hundreds of books were published in Orwell's time about the plight of miners. Orwell's is one of the very few that is still in print.

~~~~~~~~~

It might seem unfair to compare a student essay to one by Orwell. It is not. The only valid standard of writing is fine writing. It is the same for everyone. There is no lesser standard, only a lessening of the standard itself, and the best schools see themselves as maintaining a hard line on writing. Expository Writing at Harvard has described itself as, "Since 1872, the one academic experience required of every Harvard student." Good writing is, in fact, the portal of entry into the life of the university, which is why the admissions essay in which you present yourself congruently, openly, and knowledgeably, will, in one form or another, always be important, because it shows who you are. Combining the two valences seen above in Orwell, the valence of close observation and the valence of careful, almost hesitant, thought, is also, necessarily, the aim of a good admissions essay.

~~~~~~~~~~

Here is another student's essay. Imagine yourself as an admissions officer, reading it after reading the other one:

I was eating a cold orange for breakfast. Cold oranges are tough and not quite round, the way the earth is tough and not quite round. The knife my mother gave me was dull, so I went and found a sharper one in a drawer and made a slice in the orange.

I wish I could say what I saw then, but I saw it all in a moment, a seeing that was also a thought. The cut in the orange made a crescent. Some juice seeped out and pooled over the cut in three or four puddles. The puddles looked like the shape of the islands in Japan. I knew their names, Kyushu, Honshu, Shikoku, and Hokkaido, because I had recently done a report for Mr. McMurty's geography class.

More came to me: the zest was the crust. The pulp was the upwelling asthenosphere. The general shape of Japan, curled around the coast of China, was the scar of the subduction zone that has created the Japanese archipelago. In an instant I saw why form had shape. The morphology of forces in the earth had come together and made a crooked chain of islands!

Of course, I knew it was a little more complicated than this. I had studied some geology and knew the names of the layers of the earth. But I had never felt the layering from the inside. Now I did. I see now that I had had the essential thought of plate tectonics, the feeling of the knife of one plate digging into the zest of another. It was a thought in three dimensions, and it occurred to me that something like this thought must have occurred to Dietz and Hess, who originated plate tectonics in the early 1960s. I remember holding the orange in my hand, turning it on its axis. I remember trying to get it at just twenty-three and a half degrees. Could I do a half by eye?

When I had that thought, Could I do a half by eye? I knew then and there I had to study geology in college. That I had it in me to. That I felt in myself an intuition about calculations as they related to the earth. Math, for the first time, in the inner exactness of its geophysical application, seemed real to me. I started to get interested in the shapes of crystals.

What a distance from the first passage! Here, we see a complete integration of voice, a loss of the discrepancy between the writer who experiences and the writer who writes. The accumulation of statements seen in the earlier example disappears. In its place is a voice that speaks with unblocked ease. There is a looseness of movement from sentence to sentence. The sentences seem to dissolve into one another like a solid phasing into a solute, and yet there is an overall realness, culminating in a little epiphany. Behind the words one senses a real person, living, observing, thinking. It is not that the passage is closely reasoned. It is associative in method and provisional in conclusion, and the writer seems perfectly at ease with the limitations of the central association, the orange with the earth. But the writer has learned to write in such a way as to be open to experience, to new ways of seeing and understanding the world.

There is also a lovely sense of the oddities of experience. To think that the writer saw the world in an orange! Though there is a little figurative language in the passage, the writer avoids being overtly literary. The one string of metaphors is consistently drawn and follows a train of thought. The writer never actually articulates the governing simile, "the earth is like an orange." Nor is it stretched into a metaphor, "the earth is an orange." No, the comparison is quietly there, an effortlessly drawn, though approximate, equivalence in which the writer is perfectly comfortable with the fact that the earth is not an orange and is willing to laugh about even having the thought that it might be. This willingness to laugh at oneself, to think about one's perceptions and yet not take all of them seriously, is a hallmark of maturity. Mature construings of meanings are provisional, always capable of being modified by new experience, which, far from threatening, can be fun.

And yet the writer claims none of these things. The things I have observed are quietly there by implication. Crucially, the writer does not seem to have a sophistication beyond seventeen years. An adult could not possibly have written this. The ghostwritten essays I have seen over the years usually avoid flightiness or any kind of impressionism, so in this case, one can be fairly certain that a seventeen-year-old wrote it. Certainly, the writer is no trained geologist. The ideas in the passage have little fixity. There are several threads that flow from one to the next, but in them, one has the sense that feeling and thought are conjoined, that the self of the writer is a thinking self, composed but in motion, moving freely among the changing impressions thrown out widely by life. More than anything else, we take from this passage a feeling of readiness as, with quiet pleasure, the young writer approaches the next stage of life.

~~~~~~~~

The voice on display in this example has a number of other technical characteristics, each of which we shall meet with in various forms throughout this book. I will deal with each of them in their turn later on. They go to thought at the level of conception—in word, sentence, and paragraph, the basic units of expression in writing. They also go to a certain care in closely observing the world. But the crucial moment is always an integration of voice in which what the writer is trying to say, and how it is said, become one. Seeing, feeling, and thinking become conjoined. The parts become a whole.

It is true that relatively few students get to this point with their writing, even in college. But the few who do generally find themselves at the best schools in the country. Not always right away, of course.

Many students have to postpone their ambitions a few years just to catch up. Intellectual maturity is hard-won in a culture that has made an apotheosis of adolescence. Mastering the elements of prose is an irregular process that advances and retreats. There is no quick purgative for poor language and thin thought. It cannot happen in weeks or even months. Tutorial at Harvard, culminating in the senior thesis, lasts three years. It turns out that integrating your voice, learning to give relative weight and intensity to the elements that feel most yours, is a project that broadens to cover more and more territory.

~~~~~~~~~~

The mind is restless. Prose is composed. The art of writing is to hold on to something of the truth of this restlessness within a frame of composure. In preparing for admissions, this involves maintaining an honesty about where one is and about not pretending to be what one is not. Few eighteen-year-olds are or ever were mature thinkers, though many are well on their way. To become responsibly self-directed in the intellectual sense takes a very long time, and to be fair, most admissions committees are looking only for early signs of emergence. In my practice, I have found that it takes at least six months for a student to even begin to come into his or her own as a writer. Much has to be countered or reversed. Many students have learned to write merely by grafting a certain order of presentation onto the loose flow of their thoughts. They have learned to cloak their feelings in a rhetoric of argument. High school debate is just this, a structure of positions lightly held, opinions about some prospective future, set into opposition against each other. It is both simple and vague. Simple in that only two positions are carved out, and vague in that both apply to a prospective and indeterminate future.

Again, our two essays are exemplary. The first writer writes about the future in a vague and speculative way, the second about the past in a concrete and straightforward way. The university itself is overwhelmingly concerned with the past. Every field has its own classics. Even a scientific experiment is set up carefully so it can be analyzed after the fact. An event must be safely in the past before meaning can be drawn from it. Meaning sets slowly like concrete poured into a dam, which does not harden for a very long time. One of my students, coming back from college, said of her teachers at Yale, "They all live in the past, don't they?" I told her they have to. Immediate experience is powerful but unreliable. Great writers have long known this. Wordsworth once called poetry "the spontaneous overflow of powerful feelings," carefully qualifying this by going on to say that "it takes its origin from emotion recollected in tranquility." The key is recollection. Recollection, though removed, is not remote. It stands at some distance from the immediate present so as to see the present for what it was, functioning both as a memory, a recollecting, and a gathering—a re-collecting of data involving the thing remembered. It is receptive in a way that the experience of the moment is not, especially when the moment itself, coming always as a part of a compressed succession of moments, one nearly on top of the other, seems to explode with significance.

Not that I want to give the impression that practiced writers always make sound choices in this tranquil state. Not at all. An integration of voice entails a movement toward autonomy and great freedom of expression. Both, inevitably, entail great responsibility. The writer must see that writing has consequences. The writer first takes responsibility for what is said by taking responsibility for the way it is said. Then the writer learns to become responsible for every little inference that may be drawn from what has been written. Then the writer decides which reverberations (down to the most distant) have meaning and which do not. In this, the writer is self-directing, of course, but also continuously self-correcting. The process can be fraught with error, and in its early stages the writer has little confidence in the final outcome. It can be very sobering to see what one has written in the light of day.

Fortunately, there is a way forward. It involves a mastery of the basic elements of words, sentences, and paragraphs. Each derives from your sense of language. This statement may seem surprising. Why your language, after all, rather than what you say? The answer is, quite simply, because the admissions essay is necessarily short. A reader of these essays takes measure of you by first taking measure of your sense of words, sentences, and paragraphs, by which I mean, not just your ability to mass them together but your inner sense of them. What you say in an essay matters cumulatively, of course, especially when you are telling your own story, but a reader first reacts to *how* you are telling it. Do the words seem to be your own, not just in the sense of you having written them but in the sense of you having owned them individually? Are the words you use beautiful, sharp tools with which you consciously shape a sentence? Or cheap, dull implements that cut with a blunt edge? Is your sense of language casual, a matter of common usage? Or deeply deliberate, where the reader feels that you have weighed your words carefully? The answers to these questions are composed from your own sense of language, which is the very ground of your essay, and creates a sense of yourself essential to being seen in three dimensions by admissions committees.

Your sense of language goes to the same three processes we have already seen at work: seeing, feeling, and thinking.

Seeing goes to immediacy of perception and its solid building blocks of being, which are words.

Feeling goes to the beat of the sentence and to its origin in experience.

Thinking goes to the binding force of organization, which is the paragraph.

The crucial moment is an integration of voice in which what the writer is trying to say, and how it is said, become one. The parts become a whole. Word, sentence, and paragraph fuse and become the real presence of a writer.

This presence is built, piece by piece, word by word, sentence by sentence, paragraph by paragraph. We will look at each in turn.

2

Words

WORDS ON a page have being. Until you know this, know it so well that your knowledge of it is almost a feeling, you will not be able to write a reverberative sentence.

I have spoken about what the word "voice" means to me. When I hear it, I feel it steeping in me. Why? The word certainly has a meaning apart from me, a meaning in a dictionary that goes something like, "the tone or style of a form of speech or writing." But the word also has a beat just for me. Voice seems to me to have a particular grain to it, the way wood has grain. I would take this even further. Wood has a grain that appears only when it has been carefully cut by a trained worker in wood. Grain is the wood in itself, seen at the right angle, which is similar to what Michelangelo said when, looking at a block of stone, he began to see a sculpture taking shape within the stone. The work in wood or stone to be created is both there, waiting to be found, and not there, because, without the right kind of looking, it could just as easily not be found. Voice is for me this potential order or pattern we can find in our own experience. It takes a disciplined effort to find it. But when we find it, it is not an alien substance. It has a warmth to it the way wood has. It is friendly.

This is what I mean when I say all words have being. The words I choose to use have a quiet intimacy to them. I have come to see most words as potential friends, though I have at times been slow in coming to form a friendship with them.

How does one go about befriending them?

~~~~~~~~~~

Finding the right words involves a change in the manner of knowing them. Words, as words, must come into individual focus. They must come together in seeing, feeling, and thinking.

All three conditions must be met. A word must refer to something lived, to what one has felt about it, and to what one has thought about it. These three conditions— seeing, feeling, and thinking—form a unity, allowing the word to be fully welcomed into one's life, becoming at last a major reference for the person using it. The process can be compared to putting weight on a scale. The more a word is known, the heavier it becomes. As they become writers, my students mostly begin again to read very slowly. The heaviness of the words they are taking on slows down reading. Increasingly, there is a sense of self-awareness about the choosing of words. Once one knows a few words very intimately, others also become potentially knowable in an equally intimate way. A feeling for words always comes from using words with feeling. An overly objective sense of words, though desirable in certain scientific contexts, always has a certain coldness to it. Good writing is intimate. Think again of the essay about cutting the orange or Orwell's essay about the miners with blue scars on their faces. In each case, seeing leads to feeling leads to thinking—seamlessly.

~~~~~~~

The condition of experience would seem to be the easiest to meet. After all, the student in West Virginia and George Orwell in England's coal measures were both able to go and see miners coming out of a mine. But something in the seeing of the student was flawed. Look again at this sentence from the first essay:

They looked tired.

There are three words in this sentence. It has a simple structure of statement that belies how little it actually yields. Take "they." "They" are the miners, of course. All of them, taken together. There is no visual sharpness here, just the sense of a group, which is, after all, as we have seen, just how this writer construes things.

This is perception as a lump sum, and moving on to the next word, "looked," it may not even be reliable. "Looked" is used in the sense of "appeared," which also carries the sense that things might just not be as they appear. It gives the statement a slight inner hesitancy. Instead of sharpening it, the blur of the first word becomes more blurry. Only the third word, "tired", is, at last, something. It is simple and evocative and probably true. It also is the only one of the three words that could be deepened. Though the word itself is vague, it has a world of potential descriptions underneath it. The miners' faces, their way of walking, their deportment, their manner of speech—all are potentially recoverable from this word. It is quite limited, as used. But it is a good start.

~~~~~~~~~

Words come to us one at a time. It is possible to build a partly good sentence that includes a few words that have genuine reverberative depth. Certainly in the sentence, "They looked tired," the most promising word of the three is "tired." It has in it the writer's experience of seeing that the miners are tired. What remains now is to draw out the thing or things seen, using other words as evocative as "tired" but more powerfully precise. I want to go over several possibilities. Here is a first:

One man walked slowly, tiredly, sweating even though he seemed cold.

Here, a simple antithesis works wonders. The miner is both hot and cold. This only seems paradoxical until you realize that, deep in the earth, mines are hot even on a winter's day. And so does the use of "tired" as an adverb, which makes it descriptive of motion rather than fixity. The other simple improvement is that the writer now sees another person individually. For all we know, all the miners are sweating in the cold. But for the writer at this moment, only this one is. It also opens up to the writer the possibility of further description, which is always much easier to do in the singular than the plural. It opens up to the writer the great and beautiful realm of specificity. The writer could now look at his clothing, or even, one might hope, his face.

Here is a second possibility:

He was tired in his eyes, and his limbs, covered with coal dust along with the rest of his body, seemed to hang from him like black branches from a tree in the dead of winter.

Simile and metaphor always move us a little away from the actual and the concrete but not in a dangerous way, for the aim is always to bring us back to them. Here, the slight distancing effect of the simile, "like a tree," is softened by the initial concreteness of his sentence. Notice how "tired" is no longer general but specific to his eyes. The beautiful thing about a well-chosen simile or metaphor is that the image of the tree, though for a moment it leads the mind away from the miner, turns it back to him by establishing an equivalence. The "like" of the simile makes it clear that the equivalence is only tentative, avoiding the tendency of metaphor to collapse one thing into another, as in "the miner was a tree." Sometimes, having read a metaphor, it takes quite some time to get back the ground of the real, which is why novelists, concerned with reality, use them sparingly when they use them at all. Some, like Jane Austen, mostly avoid them. Our writer reaches only for a simile, traditionally a more conservative choice, rather than a metaphor, and confines it to a comparison which, on the possible spectrum of comparison, is not far-fetched at all. In fact, in winter, black, bare trees mostly surround the mines of West Virginia. Our writer's comparison has the effect of making the miners part of a landscape. The comparison is also, in a lovely way, very economical, because it evokes the landscape by implying it, giving the sentence a double force.

~~~~~~~~~~

The second condition of a word's being, feeling, presupposes that of observation. Observation has concreteness. Feeling adds an emotional dimension to it.

But the feeling must be honest. One's feelings are only one's own. A writer must be careful not to project his or her own feelings onto others or even assume that their feelings are easily transparent to an observer. Some of this projection and interpretation is, of course, inevitable, especially for the writer of fiction, but a good writer tries to own his or her feelings as much as possible. Orwell's reaction to the miners of West Riding is so effective because he acknowledges it to be fully his own. Here is our sentence, revised with feeling:

I was already tired, because getting to the mine wore me out before I even got there, winding into the mountains on a road too narrow for the big bus from suburban Philadelphia, afraid at nearly every turn of plunging into the little wrecked valleys, each a kind of garbage dump in its own right, full of twisted metal and splintered wood.

See first who is tired here. The writer is. See, too, how the writer does not presume anything about anyone else's experience. The writer stays within an individual field of vision but without a sense of confinement of observation. This is because, well-settled in a vantage point, the writer is now able to closely observe the world and react to it with feeling. In one sentence we may now pick up many glints of who the writer is. Readers are always on the lookout for these little pieces of partial knowledge they can grasp onto, and in one long sentence, we really get a sense of who the writer is and why the writer might be there. And yet there is not one declarative statement in it! The sentence succeeds primarily by suggestion. Good writing often does. It has just the right thickness of realism. I have often had the thought that good prose is a judicious layer of paint on a piece of wood. The paint is not too thin or too thick. It covers it just enough to show the grain of the wood, and even to bring it out a little. A heavy layer of paint would only destroy this effect, covering the grain, making one see the paint rather than the wood. This sentence now says enough, but not too much. It leaves room for the wood to breathe.

~~~~~~~~~

It might seem strange that I come to thinking last. Many people feel that in writing, they are thinking first. Yes, but only apparently. Thinking is simply the condition of writing of which we are the most conscious—its highest visible point. A thought is never solely a thought because it already has a large base of observations and feelings leading up to it. The problem is that many of these experiences and feelings are often partly unconscious. The truth is that, even in memory, one retains only a little of what one has actually seen and felt, and without the effort to write it down, much of it could just as easily have been forgotten or remembered only in fragments. Coming at it from the ground up, the act of writing works to elicit these unconscious, as well as nearly unconscious, observations and feelings by using words as a catalyst to a fuller awareness. For it turns out that knowing what one sees, and what one feels, is always a precondition to finding out what one thinks. The first stages of the process, leading to the stage of thought, provide a sense of the ownership of the thought that is often lacking in beginning writers. We read with a sense that a particular thought, far from being imposed on a scene, has grown out of it. A thought itself begins to be expressed as an owned feeling in terms closer to its immediate experiencing.

Here, back at the mine, is the beginning of one such rooted thought:

I had expected the mine to be a wreck, but I did not in any way foresee the radiating circles of wreckage overlapping miles and miles away; the land was tired, or worse, exhausted.

The writer pays tribute to the word "tired" by coming to the end of it. The scene passed through is more than tired. Thinking it through, a more vivid word comes to mind: exhaustion. The writer is right. The coal lands of West Virginia are an exhausted landscape. The coal tipples are mostly derelict, and most of the mines have been abandoned. In one beautiful word, the writer comes to the hard reality of what is seen. It enables the essay to move, in the very next sentence, into an idea that completes the thought:

The scene reminded me, oddly enough, of the Jersey Meadowlands, that tired belt of industrial blight I pass through every time I drive into New York City; I saw now how the one really presupposes the other, the alertness of New York City needing the exhaustion of the Meadowlands, and that both probably require West Virginia, which feeds its hungry power plants with coal heaped in hoppers along the tracks lining the New Jersey Turnpike.

Everything is now here. An experience of seeing, a sense of slight revulsion at what is seen, and a clear, focused thought about it. Note that in the merger of the three, there is an incompletion to each of them. The sentence is part observation, part feeling, and part thought. In the word "hungry" it is all three. It is effective as a unity, and it also gives the writer many places to go with it. Each of its tendrils of association can be developed in ensuing sentences. See, too, how tiredness is used here. It becomes a feeling element of the landscape as seen by the writer, and it becomes the first of two words in an escalating thought, as the sense of tiredness leads to the sense of exhaustion. An observation becomes a feeling, which becomes a thought!

~~~~~~~~~~

I began by saying that words have being. Now I can say more precisely that words have observation, feeling, and thought—and that, taken together, these are the conditions of a word's being, and a word reverberates with them. A word is perceived as having being because a reader senses these things behind it. "Tired" becomes something seen, something felt, something thought. It is not always possible, of course, to become acquainted with all the elements of a word's being in the order in which I have presented them here, even for such a simple word as "tired." One has to live a word in its varying degrees of intensity before one discovers that the being of the word is in all these things. Ideally, a writer will take on a word without knowing exactly where it will lead. We see this happening above as an ordinary word like "tired" takes on circle after circle of meaning. Both the precision of plain description, and the sharp imprecision of simile and metaphor, become available to the writer. The word as finally used may support none of the definitions in the dictionary, while crossing freely among them. What matters is that, in the end, each word becomes an intimacy with quiet inner referents readers can sense. Words lose their distant quality and, at last, become friends.

3

Sentences

Tʜɪs ꜰɪɴᴅɪɴɢ of a word, and a letting of it into one's life, is one of the deepest experiences of writing. But it is only a beginning. A word may have a great deal of meaning for me without having any real meaning for anyone else. If I simply wrote the word "voice" on the page, a reader would have no sense of all the things it meant to me. It takes a sentence to convey the pattern, the underlying order, to be found in words. A word contains, but a sentence *conveys*. A word may have the beat of observation and feeling for a writer, but only in the sentence does it begin to have the chance to convey observation and feeling to someone other than the writer. This is why, at the outset, I said that the sentence is the unit of feeling. In and of themselves, words are intransitive. It is the sentence that sets them into motion and invests them with warmth. To be effective, the individual words in the sentence must have being for the writer. But a good sentence goes further, establishing a safe harbor for its words, while allowing them potential access to the larger body of thought that is the paragraph.

~~~~~~~~~~

If a word has being, a sentence has a way of being. It seems almost to be listening to something, not in a distant way but as though it is thoroughly at home in it. This sense of *home* is vital here. It means that the writer is living thoroughly in the world he or she is writing about. There is an ease of moving around in it, which comes from a deep sense of familiarity. This can only come from a finely tuned understanding of something. This understanding may only be tentative, often involving a frequent checking as to the accuracy of what is seen, in which case the sentence gives off an air of trying to understand something rather than having understood it. Or it may be more complete, but if so, it never loses the sense of strangeness, as though the writer, while being at home in that world, is still capable of being surprised by it.

This sense of being also involves sensing the presence of the writer behind the text. I for one have never believed the critical commonplace that texts fully separate themselves from their writers. A Dickens novel always feels to me like Dickens dictating from his podium; a Mark Twain novel like Mark Twain standing over my shoulder, cracking jokes; a Henry James novel like Henry James adding his winding appositives in longhand. I find I even read Homer wondering who he was. This is because the sentences have such a distinctive way of being. The writer observes without being entirely effaced as an observer. We have been so frequently lectured on the benefits of disinterested observation that we have lost the sense of interested observation that gives a good sentence its distinctive way of being. For it is at the level of the sentence that we first begin to sense the integration of all the elements of a writer's voice, in seeing, feeling, and thinking. A sentence's way of being is seeing and feeling and thinking working in concert with a sense of being at home in a subject.

It may seem surprising that I am emphasizing nearly nonverbal aspects of sentences. But over and over again I have seen how much they matter. Though rarely spoken about directly, this dimension of feeling also plays a very large role in college admissions. A reader on a committee gets a feeling about a writer. Over and over again I have seen students get into a school, or not get in, because of how a committee, collectively, *felt* about them. I would not have written this book unless I believed that, in the end, much of this burden of representing feeling lies in the student's own hands. The grain of the individual sentence is where a reader first begins to get a sense of the writer as a person. This sensing of the feeling presence of a writer is not the same as academic performance or intellectual competence. Rather, it goes to a sense of warmth, by which I mean a special investment of the writer with the reader in a common project of inquiry. A reader should be a party to the sentence, feeling its awareness unfold as though part of the reader's own thought. In this way a sentence is fully accepted, *taken in*. Then, a reader, trusting the writer, can move beyond it to the thought of the sentence or in the direction of the thought to which the sentence is taking the reader. Again, it is the feeling of the sentence that helps to move it forward. The strength of a good sentence to create and maintain the identity of its writer needs to be seen to be appreciated, and it is to that work that I now turn.

Sentences convey by moving the reader through a succession of words. They have a specific weight given them by the words and by how they are arranged. A sentence can be heavy or light, depending on how much it takes on in seeing, feeling, and thinking. The more a writer tries to do in a given sentence, the heavier it becomes, and the harder it is for the reader to move through it to the next sentence. This does not necessarily come down to mere length. A short sentence containing a brief, abstract thought can be as confusing as a long one. A good sentence should be an exercise in moderation. Taking on only what it needs to, it moves into another sentence before becoming too unwieldy. Most sentences see or feel or think. Many see but only hint at feeling or thinking. A sentence that does all of these at the same time usually has to be built up to and is the result of careful plotting. The inflection of the word "hungry," seen in the previous chapter, is effective because its different meanings have all been sounded out in the sentences leading up to it. In this way most sentences perform a work of preparation. They are in reality helping sentences leading to a main one, just as a helping verb modifies a main verb.

Many of my students write sentences very poorly when they begin working with me. They often *think* they are good writers of sentences, and in many cases, they have been praised for writing them in high school. To teach them to write well I first have to get them to write sentences very simply. A good sentence can always be made longer, but a bad one usually needs to be thrown out. Good sentences have a hard core of good grammar. The sense of causality that is basic to our language—its fundamental structure of subject, verb, and object—gives even the simplest sentences a bedrock of good expression. Being a good writer is not a quest after a perfection of expression. It is finding the line of *good enough* and crossing it to clarity. The first essay about the mine is not completely bad, and the second essay about the orange is not completely good. But of course, there remain marked differences, and many of these go to the formation of sentences themselves.

Our two writers go about forming their sentences very differently. Here are two representative sentences taken from different parts of the two applications:

[From the first essay] *Social justice is a mountain to be climbed.*

[From the second essay] *I did not go to a science museum until I was sixteen, though my father, who was a sign painter who also painted little pictures of baby animals on rocks he sometimes sold at street fairs, knew I was interested in rocks and was always intending to take me to one someday.*

The first sentence has two parts. The first is the received idea, taken for granted, of social justice. The second is a received phrase, the cliché, vaguely biblical but really too vague to be genuinely biblical, that there is a mountain to be climbed. It is a sentiment composed of preexisting parts. Others could have been chosen and more or less dropped in without any real change in emphasis: "Social justice is a wall to be scaled" or "Oppression is a hill to be moved." When anything will do, nothing does anything. It really comes down to who is doing the forming; the writer, or some other form of agency such as a received idea or a received phrase, commonly a cliché. These preformed phrases take away any feeling of direct experience. Seeing, feeling, and thinking are far away as language takes over in its capacity as a machine. Slight deviations in phrase or tone may conceal this, but the expression is no less mechanical. Here, the writer has simply chosen *not* to form a sentence on his or her own. There are few solid points of reference here, and a reader is likely to read the sentence with a vague feeling of having seen them before in someplace or other. This is because the sense of reference, so precious in language well handled, is lost. Overall, we have a sense of unawareness pivoting awkwardly on a bad mount.

The second sentence has a simplicity of address. The *I* makes no large claims that cannot be traced to a point of origin in a single person. The first phrase implies a childhood of modest origins, though of course, the reader might later learn otherwise. The writer might possibly be from an affluent family where a formal cultural life was given little emphasis, in which case the story to be told would be very different, though equally interesting. This writer's father turns out to have been a sign painter who also paints "little pictures of baby animals on rocks." This one lovely detail opens a whole reality to a reader. These pictures are usually sentimental, realistic, and rendered in as humanly a way as possible. They are popular because they present an ideal picture of the animal world seen in human terms. This form of representation has no range and little depth, but the writer does not use the detail to criticize maudlin art. The writer uses it to show what the writer's father was like. He had aspirations. He painted signs for a living but tried his hand at art. He wanted to take his children to a museum but probably could not afford it. The writer feels no need to establish distance from the subject by saying his father was naive or that his art was mediocre. Instead the facts speak for themselves as a story. Readers are used to grasping at the thin threads of story given them to make up a narrative. In this way story is a very effective way of using small details because it relies on the reader's willingness to fill in the blanks. This sentence works as well as it does because it draws in the reader to read *with* it. Good writers use their readers' imaginations. A reader is here drawn into the world of the sentence, a companion in reading with the writer rather than merely an object of address.

The two sentences have been formed in radically different ways. One sees, and the other is seen. The seeing sentence comes from a person. The seen sentence has already been seen many times and is being repeated as a way for the writer to assert a political affiliation with other people, who may often repeat it in similar terms.

I have dwelt so long on this problem of formation because I see it as a highly crucial one. A writer who lacks an immediate experiencing of the world will tend toward an unawareness in expression. The simplest way of describing this lack of awareness is by saying that the writer lacks a full experiencing of what is seen, thought, and felt at a given moment. Everything remains external. Gaining this awareness is no easy thing. Examples (I give some below) help. But unless students begin to perceive writing as an internal problem in awareness, it will remain largely an unconscious reorganization of received ideas and phrases. This is where I find it takes a highly particular event as a point of reference, an event which can be returned to again and again, if necessary, to discover more about it. The first experiencing of it may not prove to be the best one, but in returning to it, a sharpness starts to emerge.

This is just what happens to our second writer. Something *happens*, and the writing preserves a record of it:

The knife my mother gave me was dull, so I went and found a sharper one in a drawer and made a slice in the orange. I wish I could say what I saw then but I saw it all in a moment, a seeing that was also a thought. The cut in the orange made a crescent. Some juice seeped out and pooled over the cut in three or four puddles.

The puddles looked like the shape of the islands in Japan.

The first thing we sense here is that the writer has a basic trust in his or her own awareness. The writer never once makes a secondhand claim. In this sense, the subject of an admissions essay always has to be an *I*. Any movement away from the first person presents dangers for the inexperienced writer. Even if the *I* is not present in the subject position, it needs to be there. The *I* can actually be located anywhere in the sentence or not be there at all. Look at these sentences from Orwell's *Homage to Catalonia*:

I seldom fired my rifle; I was too frightened of the beastly thing jamming . . . [w]e had tin hats, hardly any revolvers or pistols, and not more than one bomb between five or ten men. The bomb in use at this time was a frightful object known as the "FAI" bomb, it having been produced by the Anarchists in the early days of the war. It was on the principle of a Mills bomb, but the lever was held down not by a pin but by a piece of tape.

In the first sentence the *I* is clearly present. Orwell is scared of his rifle. The second continues the perception within the governing frame of the *I*, just extending it to speak of himself as a member of a small group, a *we* of soldiers poorly equipped. The next sentences use neither *I* nor *we* but are placed there to explain his immediate experience with his equipment. In the last sentence, we may seem far from the *I*, but a small marker such as a lever of a bomb held down "not by a pin but by a piece of tape" has the feel of close, intimate observation.

Every sentence in an admissions essay tilts around the axis of the *I*. Sentences that lack any sense of a personal marking are likely to become unmoored. To return to a draft of our essay at the mine:

I saw the miners, their faces dirty with coal, and thought how social justice needed to be done for all in America, black and white, gay and straight, manager and worker, and that the social will to change would have to be organized at the grassroots.

See first how long this sentence is. A very long sentence strays far from its core. In practiced hands, long sentences can be beautiful, but students writing for admission to college are mostly very unpracticed writers. The core here is a writer, seeing in the first person. But the longer the sentence gets, the more abstract it becomes.

Ideas thicken a sentence and slow it down even if it is of middle length. A long thick sentence is the very worst kind, heavy and dragging like the one above. I tell my students to keep to the core of English grammar, the simple structure of subject, verb, and object. The subject is the doer, the verb the action, the object the target of the action. In rewriting, long sentences should be divided up to see what they look like:

I saw the miners, their faces dirty with coal. Social justice needed to be done for all in America, black and white, gay and straight, manager and worker. The social will to change would have to be organized at the grassroots.

Gone is the false appearance of cause. Separated, the sentences now stand as what they are, unaligned fragments of seeing and feeling and thinking. Usually, only the beginning is useable, for it alone relies on something seen. In contrast, the other parts of the sentence become assertions that have to be taken almost on faith. Beginning writers often come up with long trains of sentences like this one, where the middles and ends of the sentences are like boxcars coupled to a distant locomotive. Here, the observation of the dirty faces of the miners, good in itself, pulls a train of clichés behind it. Nothing about the sentence is unexpected. The observation is far from Orwell's observation of seeing the blue scar at the mine. The ideas themselves are a typical list of vague student demands, none of which are indexed to the actual reality of the miners. Simple sentences, with

their simple grammar, restrain the writer. The longer
the sentence gets, the greater the risk of writing a bad
one. It is not so much a case of jumping to conclusions
as pulling them along as dead weight. By contrast, the
I is never dead. Its presence revitalizes and keeps the
writer grounded in personal experience. Most students
can readily see how a simple causal version of one of the
abstractions above—

I plan to see to it that social justice is done.

—is a ridiculous overstatement.

    I almost never have to teach my students grammar.
I have to teach them restraint. Getting to know words,
they feel their power and start to use them, heavily but
loosely, as in this writer's use of the word "justice." The
problem with the above sentence is not that it is poorly
written. It is that it has a massively overinflated sense
of the writer's own power. The *I* goes too far. It assumes
that wanting to do something is the same as doing it.
It confuses intention with action, with the result that
the action itself is occluded. "I plan to see it" is a massive overvaluation of the writer's own agency. This thin
assertion is almost immediately undercut by the plan
itself, to see that "social justice is done," placed almost
necessarily in the passive voice, because underneath the
statement the writer really knows that he or she has
little power beyond an ability to assert it in language.
Indeed, there is something childish here, a wish lurk-
ing under it for an all-powerful force to which one can

look for protection, a force that has a magical character such as a belief in "social justice." Language here does little for the writer other than making large, impersonal forces personal, whereas the truth of writing is that the writer is only one person, writing, with a heavy awareness of being only one. Here are a few such reminders with commentary:

So, we fly home. On the plane a heavy woman, a spinster, perhaps a schoolteacher, with flying gray hair, who takes from her pocketbook a dozen glass animals she bought in Venice and, unwrapping them one by one, holds them up to the light.

—JOHN CHEEVER

Here, the sentence sees. It closely observes a real scene—a woman on a plane, traveling alone, looking over souvenirs she bought in Venice. Cheever tells us she is a spinster but shows us her essential loneliness by letting us see with what care she handles her precious mementoes. "Flying" gray hair is a lovely image that begins, ever so gently, to capture a sense of her yearning. See too how a sentence grounded in close observation can often be a little longer than one expressing a thought. The reader does not mind the length because the sentence is filling in a picture until it is complete.

And now I have a multitude of pleasant jobs on hand, & am really very busy, & very happy, & only want to say Time, stand still here; which is not a thing that

many women in Richmond could say I think. Nessa &
I are collaborating over a paper for cover which she has
designed, & I am to colour.

—VIRGINIA WOOLF

Here, the sentence climaxes in feeling, but see first
how grounded it is in close observation, though in this
case, the details come at the very end. The feeling also
tilts into a thought, the idea of time standing still. This
thought is anything but abstract. As soon as Woolf has
it, she thinks of the many other women living in Richmond, laboring unhappily, doing unsatisfying work.
This passage is from her *Diary*. Observe how its short-
hand actually adds to its feeling, giving it a quality of
breathlessness.

No one wants to be a prisoner; you don't have to be; and
so William Holden escapes easily. On the Kwai, hun-
dreds tried; most of them were killed; no one succeeded.

—IAN WATT

Here is thought in action. These two sentences are so
plain they are almost muscular. The myth and its corrective are set in careful parallel. They come from an
essay called "The Bridge on the River Kwai as Myth."

Watt had been imprisoned by the Japanese during
World War II and had helped build the famous bridge.
I took a seminar from him at Stanford on the novels
of Joseph Conrad. He barely spoke. He often gave the
impression that ordinary speech was so inexact that it

was mostly painful for him to hear. He had a reluctance to speak, as though speech was to him far more important than he could possibly say, and each word he said had to be earned. Watt's writing has that quality of *necessary* speech. When he wrote there was a sense that he saw what he saw so clearly that he *had* to say it, if only as a corrective to those around him who were slow to see what had presented itself to him with such clarity as an integrated moment of experience in observation, feeling, and thought.

I found I was almost always wrong where it was possible to be wrong.

—GEORGE ORWELL

My own favorite, completely self-explanatory, placed on a card above my desk at home.

~~~~~~~~~

The claims these sentences make are modest. Gone is the distant court of social justice that will act with complete power and wisdom. Instead we have a real world in which actions are limited and intentions incomplete. These writers expect very little to be explained to them. They wish to see only what they can see for themselves. They work with rough approximations knowing how rough they are, hoping not for universally valid statements but for plain statements of fact that build to a small core of knowledge from which some limited conclusions may be reached. They do not overvalue their powers of observation but return again and again to the actual events in which these observations are grounded. They have, in short, a kind of maturity of observation that often has nothing to do with writing, but which can definitely be elicited by it.

Here, I am reminded that the strongest candidates for admission are usually those who are also the most intellectually mature. Merely being intellectual is not enough. Unfortunately, there is no Piaget of intellectual development to consult here. But in my practice, I have observed certain lines of development. A maturing student no longer takes experience as received. There is a widening of the field of possible interpretation, and, at first at least, a very real confusion in the face of it. It is why it is well to begin with small, intense experiences. These at least give a real point of departure. A writer is not likely to be satisfied with a solution for them expressed in crude or global terms. The trip to the mine was one such experience, and in the case treated above, I was able to show the student how to use language itself as a way into the experience, by explaining how self-enclosed and uncommunicative certain kinds of sentences can be. A good sentence has a modesty of aim. It acknowledges the smallness of the writer while refusing to submit completely to it. It adjusts itself to reality, trying to get to know it, always checking what is felt and thought against what is seen, looking and looking again to try and miss as little as possible.

Good sentences take patience. You begin from where you are, a *here*, a *home*. You write from what you see where you live, what you feel about what you see where you live, and what you think about what you see and feel where you live. Always from *where you live*. Then, vested with a sense of home, you look at what you have written and reread it. I have done little more than that in this book so far, reading sentences carefully and seeing both what they do and what they are trying to do in the context of where a writer is really living. They too often fail to do what they are trying to do. I have learned to see that this is a failure, not so much in handling language, but in the seeing and feeling and thinking that leads up to it. Unless writing opens what William Blake once called "the doors of perception," your sentences will never say what you think they do. They will say things that can be said in language— even the most grandiose abstraction is still a statement in language—but the statement will not be your own. Language has a way of taking over the unaware writer, putting what has already been felt and seen elsewhere before what is being seen by the writer in the present moment. Language, even language actively spoken in the present moment, always has a past. It takes considerable training to know where its parts come from in the past and to sort the strong constructions from the weak, the dead matter of jargon, cliché, and rhetoric. Think of these as inscriptions on gravestones. Better to strive for the freshness of the living moment rather than entering the cemetery of language. Knowing what you see and feel and think is enough, in the moment, without all the dead weight of language's many failures. For language can fail us, and it often does when it takes the place of who we are.

Who we are. Most of my students bound for college have grammar that is already good enough. What they lack is a sense of responsibility in writing, an awareness not only of who they are but of where they are. Seeing well, feeling fully, and thinking slowly, they can use writing to broaden their field of available perception by bringing new things into their field of vision. At last, it gives students something to write *about*. A writer starts living in a subject rather than just writing about it as a distant object. Dealing with bad writing merely as a problem in conforming to certain rules of grammar or elements of style prevents the students from perceiving writing as real. Writing well must be approached first as a problem in consciousness, because only when students start to see the world in a moment of immediate, full, and acceptant experiencing do they begin to write well. George Orwell writes as well as he does because he always provides himself with solid points of reference. In *The Road to Wigan Pier*, he goes to live with miners in the north of England. In *Homage to Catalonia*, he joins the fight for Republican Spain. His writing is, in this way, a clear-cut extension of his living in a solidly defined reality.

It may seem as if my method is purely perceptual. That is, that I am arguing that a deepening of seeing leads to good writing. This is only partly true. Good writing depends on good seeing, which certainly needs to be seeded, but good seeing does not automatically make for good writing. There are three questions to be asked of each sentence:

Is the observation your own?
Is the feeling your own?
Is the thought your own?

The answer to all of them must be *yes*. It must be yes at the level of words, yes at the level of sentences, and yes, as we will see, at the level of paragraphs. If the answer is fully yes, your writing may not be good writing, let alone great writing. But it will be acceptable in some way, serviceable as seeing, and it can be made the basis of careful revision.

Revising a sentence you have not seen or felt, let alone thought, is a waste of time. Remember the order: seeing to feeling to thought. Make sure your experience is close and accurate, your feelings clear, and then the thought will follow. The weight of the observation and the clarity of the feeling flowing from it will shape the strength of the thought that follows. A thought that is flawed in observation or feeling will not hold up well under examination. One grounded in observation and feeling may or may not, depending on how it is pursued. But these are the necessary preconditions.

4

Paragraphs

So FAR, I have spoken only generally about the implications of good writing for the admissions essay. This lays the essential ground, because there is very little chance that anything other than good writing will persuade readers who, day in and day out, are looking for it as the primary mark of a promising young mind.

But the admissions essay has its own form. As a literary form it is very minor indeed, though it draws on techniques from the essay and the novel. But it has a few things that it must do, and these are particular to the form and govern the dynamics of its unfolding.

These dictates are all related to the fact that the writer approaches the reader as a complete unknown. The masthead of a well-known newspaper or the spine of an established publisher does not announce to the reader that the writer has been read. To the contrary: the writer of the admissions essay is always in the position of a young, unread writer who has to prove quickly that he or she is worthy of being read. Many young writers seem to think that a sense of sincerity will do this, and many essays adopt this tone. But sincerity is not proof of fitness for college. The ability to reason is. To reason from observation and evidence, to reason through doubt, to reason not to global conclusions but to a satisfying small statement that has at least a reasonable chance of being true. Reasoning is hesitant, provisional, cautious. It does not mask doubt but plumbs it and uses it as the basis for hard knowledge.

So, a young writer must first establish some kind of credibility, a credibility without credentials. This would seem to be almost impossible until one remembers how writing itself works. Good writing is a compound of seeing, feeling, and thinking. It is easiest to contest a thought, a little less easy to contest a feeling, and very hard to contest what is seen, especially if what is seen in recorded with a high degree of precision and accuracy in good prose. The pursuit of that prose has mostly been the subject of this book. Now I want to turn to the formal mechanics of self-presentation in the admissions essay to show how the very process of writing can be folded into the structure of an admissions essay that works by earning its credibility though a slow-building movement from seeing to feeling to thinking. There is no one set outline for this process. It has many variations. But all of them are variations on the theme of a writer who realizes that he or she has to earn the trust of a skeptical reader.

Most of the forms of written argument do not apply readily to the admissions essay. The admissions essay is not an argument for you but an extension of you, of how you see the world, into writing.

Moments of great personal insight are rarely reached by the mechanics of argumentation itself. Once you set up an argument, it becomes a machine for proving a point (which is why it is often called a *line* of argument); sometimes it is an aspect of resemblance, sometimes it is an observation of how things border in time or place, and sometimes it is an instance of cause and effect. Paragraphs structured by this logic of argumentation often have clarity without insight. There is a place for dispassionate clarity in writing, but the form of the admissions essay favors an engaged openness to the world of the writer. The logic of paragraphing often has the effect of moving the reader away from *you*. This sense of you is not the culmination of the essay but should be visible in its every sentence. There is no sense of rushing in a good admissions essay. It should have an almost leisurely pace. You are not proving a point but letting someone into your world.

In a good admissions essay, seeing leads to feeling leads to thinking. In practical terms, this often means that a first paragraph sees, a second paragraph feels, and a third paragraph thinks, and the last paragraph moves the essay to the point of action. In college essays, paragraphs work through the logical forms of resemblance, contiguity of time and place, and cause and effect. But they have no need to present self. The need to present oneself calls for a perceptual progress of paragraphs that builds a clear sense of the person narrating. Most essays unfold arguments. An admissions essay unfolds a coherent picture of the person writing it. In practice, the seeing and feeling often overlap considerably, in part, because there is often a need to anticipate what is coming. But, however configured, this is a very different demand than most students have ever met in writing, and it takes some time to get used to it.

~~~~~~~~~~

The concrete is always a good point of departure for an admissions essay. It earns trust by showing close observation reliably in action. This holds for great writers as well as for lesser ones. Here is the beginning of an essay by Elizabeth Bishop called "Gregorio Valdes":

The first painting I saw by Gregorio Valdes was in the window of a barber shop on Duval Street, the main street of Key West. The shop is in a block of cheap liquor stores, shoeshine parlors and pool rooms, all under a long wooden awning shading the sidewalk. The picture leaned against a cardboard advertisement for Eagle Whiskey, among other window decorations of red-and-green crepe-paper rosettes and streamers left over from Christmas and the announcement of an operetta at the Cuban school—all covered with dust and fly spots and littered with termites' wings.

Here, it does not matter who Elizabeth Bishop is. Right away you are in her eyes, seeing what she sees. She is in a particular place looking at something. She begins the passage with an establishing shot of the block, then moves to what she sees in the barbershop window. By the end of the paragraph, you know where she is, what kind of a place it is, and what she sees in it.

Bishop's seeing is very clear. It is important to ask why. There is always so much to be seen that any act of seeing has to be highly organized to be *seeable* by a reader. Detail must be built up. In Bishop's opening paragraph, the clarity of the scene is established one step at a time. There are three discrete planes of vision—a far plane, a middle plane, and a close plane. These are the most common focal planes of human vision, and in her paragraph, Bishop follows a normal progression of focus. First, she sees far things, all part of Duval Street, the main street of Key West. Then she moves to a middle distance, focusing on a single block of stores. Then she moves to the closest plane, seeing something, a painting in a store window. This three-plane model is often employed in art, photography, and cinema, for it synchronizes a scene with the way the eye naturally pictures it at different focal lengths. It allows for a gradual adjustment of a viewer's eyes to the scene by adding new planes of focus stepwise to what has already been seen. It is also finite. There is no large infinity of horizon or small infinity of detail. Instead, the reader pictures a scene bounded by three receding planes of focus. Undoubtedly, what Bishop records is only a small selection of what can be seen on the main street of Key West. But she records it in such a way that what she sees is communicable to a reader through the medium of highly structured prose. By seeing, Bishop brings order to what she sees. She does it again in much the same way in the following paragraph, where she uses the same three-plane model to describe a scene in Valdes' painting:

It was a view, a real View, of a straight road diminishing to a point through green fields, and a row of straight Royal Palms on either side, so carefully painted that one could count seven trees in each row. In the middle of the road was a tiny figure of a man on a donkey, and far away on the right the white speck of a thatched Cuban cabin that seemed to have the same mysterious properties of perspective as the little dog in Rousseau's The Cariole of M. Juniot.

In each sentence of the essay so far, there is a progressive movement through the planes of vision until, here, she counts seven trees. The counting is a nice touch. It gives us the feeling that she is really looking at what is in front of her and allows her, in the next sentences, to make the jump to comparing the painting in the barbershop window to a masterwork by Henri Rousseau. In this one beautiful leap, the naive observer becomes the educated critic. But she does not turn it into an exercise in art criticism. She goes back to her narrative:

The sky was blue at the top, then white, then beautiful blush pink, the pink of a hot, mosquito-filled tropical evening. As I went back and forth in front of the barbershop on my way to the restaurant, this picture charmed me, and at last I went in and bought it for three dollars. My landlady had been trained to do "oils" at the Convent.—The house was filled with copies of The Roman Girl at the Well, Horses in a Thunderstorm, *etc.—She was disgusted and said she would paint the same picture for me, "for fifteen cents."*

The painter, Gregorio Valdes, is obviously not a famous artist. But she sees something in him. Here, we see Elizabeth Bishop herself, showing what she feels by buying the painting and standing up for herself against the opinion of her landlady, who feels she could have done a better job herself. A few lines later she says it even more directly: "I liked one picture."

~~~~~~~~~~

What has happened here? Elizabeth Bishop has gone from seeing to feeling. There is a flicker of a thought based on resemblance in the comparison to Rousseau, but only in passing. The main work of the passage is for us to see the world through her eyes and to begin to trust her. Our sense of trust in her rises organically from her believability as a reliable observer. Anyone who has been to Key West has seen its slight tropical seediness. She makes no claims to seeing something new. She only records what she sees with a freshness of it unfolding in real time. There are no generalities in the passages I have quoted, and only the glimmer of an idea exists. But she, the writer, is there, and by the end of the second paragraph the sense of her *thereness* is very solid.

An admissions essay may take many forms, but in my practice, one of the most reliable opens with this sense of solidity in close observation. This usually forms the work of the first paragraph. The second paragraph continues this work by adding an overlay of feeling to seeing. The sense in the first paragraph is of a camera recording a scene. The second paragraph continues the seeing but deepens it by showing that someone, a real person, is doing the seeing. It removes any hint of coldness from the observation in the first paragraph and begins to invest the essay with a warmth by using "I." Only in the third paragraph does the sense of an idea begin to emerge, and even then, the idea is a simple, hard-won extraction:

I liked one picture of a homestead in Cuba in the same green fields, with two or three of the favorite Royal Palms and a banana tree, a chair on the porch, a woman, a donkey, a big white flower, and a Pan-American airplane in the blue sky.

It is not much of a thought, but it is the central thought of the essay, and she came to it very much on her own. Everyone she speaks to thinks little of Valdes and his art. But she likes some of it, and having shown us what she sees in him, she stands by it. The smallness of this thought—just, simply, that she likes him—is enhanced by her courage in being willing to have it. In this way she shows us just how hard it is to have a genuinely independent thought about something. The received opinion was that Gregorio Valdes was a mediocre painter of signs. It took imagination for Elizabeth Bishop to come to the idea that there was something to his work. That the idea was not complex is beside the point. It was an original idea because *she* was the first to have it, and characteristically, she tells us exactly what she likes about it in great detail.

In the same way, the thought coming out of an admissions essay need not be a high and complicated thing. It need only be your own. Bishop's thought that Valdes has something as an artist is quite limited in scope. She makes no large claims about the quality of his work. She continues to see it clearly as the essay proceeds, coming almost hesitantly to an evaluation that is thoroughly fair:

Gregorio was not a great painter at all, and although he certainly belongs to the class of painters we call "primitive," sometimes he was not even a good "primitive." His pictures are of uneven quality. They are almost all copies of photographs. . . . [But] when he copied . . . from a photograph of something he knew and liked, such as palm trees, he managed to make just the right changes in perspective and coloring to give it a peculiar and captivating freshness, flatness, and remoteness.

Her essay succeeds because she *owns* her thoughts. She shows us how they came to her and where. The final impression the essay leaves us with is that she has lived with her subject for a while, not taking one look at it but many, living nearby, looking over his pictures, buying a few, commissioning one, visiting Valdes in his home, talking to other people who knew him, crossing his world at many points before she sets pen to paper. There is no sense here, so often seen in naive admissions essays, of the one-time tourist writing up impressions of a new, strange place, usually a poor place visited for the purpose of saying it had been seen and in order to produce a record of the visit. Bishop had to have lived in Key West for a while to accumulate this portrait in depth. Her own life is not external to the life of the world around her. She wrote about Valdes because she was living her own life and his work came into it. She became interested in his work and sought him out. She did not do so simply to write about it.

The thought so expressed has an immediacy and a living fullness. She is aware of Valdes and his art but not as an object. She finds meaning in and through her experience and comes to only such ideas as seem to suit it. The thought of the essay does not come from external sources. Thought is here neither abstract nor remote, and she is not afraid of being vague when she well knows she cannot be clear, once admitting near the end that Valdes's painting is still for her "a partial mystery." In this way she accepts that a thought can have a feeling basis that often eludes a final exactness.

It may seem strange to value such an inconclusive essay and stranger still to offer it as a model for those seeking admission to college. But Bishop is a model for writers who seek to open themselves to their own experience. She looks at something that no one thinks is important and finds something of small, but real, importance to *her*. Precisely because it is important to her, and her alone, she is not going to be satisfied with an idea that levels out the more intangible elements of her experience. She does not seek to persuade anyone of anything. She never lets go of her exactness in seeing even when she is describing something that is hard to describe—and something that she is very aware that no one else sees or even thinks is worth seeing. The essay has real courage, not of conviction, which is commonly shared, but of perception, which is not. Many of my students tell me it is their favorite essay, the one among the many we read that has given them real permission to write what they saw, felt, and thought—no matter what.

~~~~~~~~~~

Let us turn and see what happens when our writer at the mine tries, like Bishop, to write what was actually seen, felt, and thought—*no matter what*. First, the *seeing*:

The Tucker & Piece coal mine was the first mine I ever saw. From the outside it looked like an empty railroad yard with a long, high conveyor belt leading into it. The road leading into it was unpaved. The mine was on a loop of the river in the Monongahela Valley, about two hours south of Pittsburgh on the school bus. On the way down my history teacher taught us an old song about Joe Hill, a miner killed in a strike at a copper mine:

Joe Hill ain't dead, he says to me
Joe Hill ain't never died
Where working men are out on strike
Joe Hill is at their side
Joe Hill is at their side

Coming out of the bus, we felt like union organizers even though we were just high school students there for a trip to Appalachia.

We never went inside the mine. I never saw any miners either. The representatives from the company had white faces and clean hands. Instead they took us to a large damp classroom, with technical diagrams on the walls, where we bought candy bars from dusty vending machines. Then they gave us a "tour" of the grounds, which took maybe twenty minutes and ended back at the room. Then one of them talked for maybe twenty more minutes about how the mine worked, mostly about the machines they used, drills and conveyor belts.

Here is the second section, equally clear, but as to what is *felt*:

My friend Seth didn't like this. He talked to a couple other kids and they started heckling him.

"Where's the mine? Why aren't you taking us there? What are you hiding? Why can't we talk to the miners?"

I joined in this, too. The representative, heavy, ruddy, his boss standing behind him, got flustered.

He stood not behind the podium but a little to the side of it. He spoke stooped, his words seeming to drop to the ground unheard. I heard little bits. "I'm glad—I serve—this facility." While he was speaking, I looked at him closely for the first time. His hand shook with notes he hardly looked at. He kept trying to meet the eye of his boss, looking for direction, but the boss kept looking away. This made him even more nervous. I saw how badly he wanted to do his job even though, with us there, it seemed he wasn't quite sure what it was. Was he supposed to defend the company? The miners? The mining of coal itself? It occurred to me that, despite what we had been told, he was not some hard corporate spokesman, but a soft man dragged from his warm office on a cold winter's day and made to speak without knowing exactly why he was speaking, or to whom.

I looked around the faces of my classmates. Most of them had been told not to like this man with a red fatty neck spilling out of his white collar, so they didn't. A low audible hissing followed his every pause.

Then I looked again. The man with the notes in his hands had tears in his eyes.

And here is the third section, where seeing and feeling are effectively translated into *thinking*:

It was all so different than what I had been told. I had been told that the people who ran the mines were,

basically, enemies of the people. Enemies of the people:
I ran over that phrase in my head, trying to remember
from my AP History class where it came from. Then I
did—it was from Stalin's purge trials of the 1930s. Oh
lord, how I shuddered when I remembered the show tri-
als and the gulags that followed.

The beauty of this response is all in one short sentence, "Then I looked again." The writer looks again,
then again, then again. Each time, the writer is forced
to revise an ongoing estimate of what has been seen,
checking it for accuracy. An initial perception may begin
as fixed but starts to be modified as soon as new facts
come pouring in, telling the writer that the "corporate
spokesman" was not as expected. The man is not a title
but a person with an inner world only partially legible
from the outside. The sight of him trips up our writer
who now has to look at the conditioned responses of the
other protestors—their hissing—with some skepticism.

So even in a group, moved by a common agenda,
our writer is driven back to an individual perception of
things, where, seeing what only *the writer as one person*
can see, he or she begins to question a comfortable belief
in the knowledge of what is right and what is wrong.

The passage also has, for the first time in this student's
writing, a climate of realness. We have already seen that
the writer at the mine managed to write the other draft
of the essay without once asking what he or she saw or
felt. But now, seeing what Elizabeth Bishop was able
to do, the writer allows an event to unfold, openly, in

real time. There is a sense of situation. This openness to the outer world leads directly to a more open inner world. What is felt is now more directly congruent with what is seen. This seeing begins with the close observation of detail but does not end with it. Our writer sees the trembling in the man's hand, sees his boss behind him, sees him trying to meet his boss's eye. Moment by moment the writer builds a detailed picture which leads to construing a feeling. The man is ill at ease. Though our writer cannot fully know exactly why, he or she can at least observe it without making judgments, and in this observation is the seed of accurate empathy. The more the writer sees, the more clearly the writer feels, and in this clarity of feeling our writer is able, finally, to become fully separate from those compatriots in the crowd who clearly view the "corporate spokesman" as less than human. By becoming more thorough in seeing, our writer becomes more thorough in feeling.

It is precisely this dual strength that gives our writer the ability to avoid having an idea about what is seen and felt that is premature. "Premature" is the perfect word here, merging as it does a rush to judgment with a sense of immaturity. The fact is that mature judgment *is* slow. By slowing down perception, our writer slows down the pace of judgment, which gives time and space to lay aside personal views and values for long enough to enter into another's world. That world may seem strange, and the writer's understanding of it may be imperfect. But it is a start, and Elizabeth Bishop has shown the way.

5

The Essay as a Whole

I HAVE TRIED to sketch, in a brief way, what happens when writers own their own experience. This process involves several lines of inquiry, separable at first, becoming more closely parallel as the process proceeds. We have seen what happens when observation and feeling and thought form a whole. What, then, does it look like when words and sentences and paragraphs come together at last and form an *essay*? How do we get from what we have learned from how to see and feel and think to the finality of words on a page? And how does the admissions essay as a whole move toward a conclusion, directed to a particular school or schools?

So far, I have used two case studies of admissions essays to clarify the outline of my approach. But giving students examples of well-crafted admissions essays is not how I actually work with them. Examples of completed admissions essays often moves them in a bad way, amplifying anxiety and encouraging imitation. Instead, I give them examples of good writing by great writers. This strategy goes to a very particular situation we find ourselves in today, for many of our students (even the best among them) actually read very little.

I was taught that one learned how to write by, first, reading. Today, it works nearly in reverse. Students have learned how to write by cultivating their own voices. Because these voices are generally oral, there is usually a pronounced orality to their writings. Many of them feel as though they have been directly dictated onto the page. Some, more or less, have. Some strains of oral storytelling can often liven prose, filling it with feeling. But *thought*, as such, does not thrive in such an oral context. In our society, the careful transmission of thought from one generation to another depends overwhelmingly on texts.

Good writing is similarly textually dependent. This is not to say that it copies texts. It is to say that, in the last instance, it depends on them for its voicing. The beat of language, as heard by the writer, has a textual inflection. The integration of voice of which I have spoken only rarely takes place orally. It takes an oral culture to create a genuinely integrated oral voice, and in many places on earth where oral cultures are still preeminent, orality is still preeminently *the* way to voice. But for my students seeking admission to the great universities, the oral often dampens the written. Writing has capabilities that go beyond mere speech, though speech can often at times offer some chance help. In this sense, it is misleading to study speeches as texts. Speeches are performances that rarely hold up to sustained close reading. They can be very compelling, lovely in their way, but in many of them, the thoughts, though overarching, are only half-formed.

It is important to give students texts that offer them a way of seeing words in addition to hearing them. Here, the choice of the text is crucial. It takes me many hours before I know enough about a student's history, intelligence, and special abilities to be able to suggest a text for study. Even then, I have to follow the student's lead and act as nondirectively as possible. It is almost never an easy learning experience, for most texts of suitable richness have a deep internal world that is not easily accessed on first reading. And most students are not open to most texts. They do not like the strings that are attached to them, the way they have of affiliating themselves, as though with invisible tendrils, to hundreds of other texts whose written lives they presume. Introducing a text to a student is, I have found, tantamount to introducing a student to the many texts underlying it. They have to like the idea of a deep and continuing communication between texts in that particular world; to be interested enough in it to read around it, until what they have read begins to appear duly three-dimensional.

To begin this work, I often choose highly personal texts by literary writers: essays, autobiography, journalism, diaries, and notebooks. These works stay close to the grain of real experience. Their inward-looking quality is balanced by a dailiness of perception, a sense of ideas dirtied in the ground of their growth. I rarely choose works of philosophical density or abstraction because students have a tendency to slip into that voice rather than their own. I prefer that they deal with ideas *in situ*, written by people who seek to draw only low-level inferences from what they see and hear. Each essay I choose is discernibly individual, not just in style but in theme, for each goes to a crucial moment in which the writer became aware of the writer's own individuality as against a received structure of thought imposed by family, region, or culture. Each describes a *freeing* of the writer. Each does so in a style that, in itself, shows that freedom in action. Together they act as a reminder that no writer starts in the world in a state of freedom. No matter where one begins, a writer's freedom is always an extraction and often an exaction, leading to the discovery of voice, moving toward its integration in a style in which seeing, feeling, and thinking interpenetrate.

Not all of these texts have to be finished examples of voice. It is not a good idea for students to look only at texts that are considered perfect. It is just as important for them to see writers as having problems to overcome, even as they themselves have problems to overcome. They need to see how frequently writers produce incomplete, ineffective, or even clumsy works.

Reading over a story that does not jell, a letter broken off midway, a diary with large gaps in it, they begin to have a feel for just how hard it is to write in a way that is close to their own experiencing, as well as for the irregularly advancing process that is writing. They can see for themselves how afraid even great writers can be to share their most intimate thoughts with their readers; locking them up in diaries, notebooks, or commonplace books because they do not wish to publish them in that incomplete form. Seeing writers at work in this way, they come to see voice not as a tight circling of identity but as an opening of identity to all that is in the world. It then becomes easier for them to accept the reality of their own groping, tentative efforts.

I could go on about these essays in the abstract, but I want to show in detail how one works. I often use essays in which a writer reaches back into his or her childhood or teenage years to see an event as both formative and directive. These essays almost all draw a clear contrast between the past and the present. They make use of all the writer's memory can supply, while recognizing, with the distance of a few years, that the writer's awareness at the time was often quite limited. In this there is always a sense of a writer *owning* an experience in all its complexity, a sense of the writer letting a story emerge from experience rather than twisting it to fit some preconceived idea. These essays usually move very slowly toward ideas, discovering the structure of the experience in the act of relating it. The ideas, once expressed, seem visceral to the essay. One might almost say that this feeling of an idea impacted in an experience is its most essential quality. Ideas then seem *lived*. One fine example of an essay closely attuned to an experience is Guy Davenport's "Finding."

Davenport opens with a memory:

Every Sunday afternoon of my childhood, once the tediousness of Sunday school and the appalling boredom of church were over with, corrosions of the spirit easily salved by the roast beef, macaroni pie, and peach cobbler that followed them, my father loaded us into the Essex, later the Packard, and headed out to look for Indian arrows. That was the phrase, "to look for Indian arrows." Children detect nothing different in their own families: I can't remember noticing anything extraordinary in our family being the only one I knew of that devoted every Sunday afternoon to amateur archeology.

The essay starts indirectly. Davenport does not launch immediately into talking about arrowheads. He talks about his Sundays. The leisureliness of his pacing is an important lesson for the college admissions essay. *Even a short essay can unfold slowly.* There is no sense of rushing to get his point across. Vivid details establish the scene as Davenport builds trust with the reader through close observation, talking about going to church, eating macaroni pie and peach cobbler (indirectly establishing the place as somewhere in the South), then piling into an old car, an Essex or a Packard (indirectly establishing the time as sometime in the 1930s). In passing he also allows us to feel an emotion, his impatience at going to church, and presents us with the very beginning of a thought he will explore later on, that children detect nothing different in their families. Seeing, he lays the ground for telling us what he feels and thinks.

It is remarkable how much work can be done in one or two sentences. Part of this work goes to how Davenport grounds his thought in seeing and feeling and continues to ground it by making the thought more personal, rather than less, as he develops it. But Davenport also gives his readers all the rudiments of a good story—setting, character, and plot. The setting is given in small details, such as peach cobbler and macaroni pie. His character is shown in how quickly he works to free himself from his church-going family; he is both part of them and apart from them. And his plot is simplicity itself: looking for arrowheads! Here, two systems of order coexist. The formal elements of story are quietly superimposed over the basic structure of seeing, feeling, and thinking. Seeing gives us a setting. Feeling gives us character. And thought gives us plot. These quiet equivalences are what account for the passage's resonance. Like a lot of great writers, Davenport does a lot here *without appearing to*. The passage has a layered quality that is almost offhand. It feels full and rich without seeming dense and heavy.

The second paragraph sharpens his feelings:

We took along, from time to time, those people who expressed an interest in finding Indian arrows. Most of them, I expect, wanted an excuse for an outing. We thought of all neighbors, friends, and business associates in terms of whether they were good company or utter nuisances on our expeditions. Surely all my attitudes toward people were shaped here, all unknowing. I learned that there are people who see nothing, who would not have noticed the splendidest of tomahawks if they had stepped on it, who could not tell a worked stone from a shard of flint or quartz, people who did not feel the excitement of the whoop we all let out when we found an arrowhead or rim of pottery with painting or incised border on it, a pot leg, or those major discoveries which we remembered and could recite forever afterward, the finding of an intact pipe, perfect celt, or unbroken spearhead elegantly core-chipped, crenelated and notched as if finished yesterday.

The value of seeing is set high here: *I learned there are people who see nothing.* Davenport continues his own loving labor of seeing, adding a sense of the excitement of the little family expeditions. His world-building is slow and visual. Tendencies emerge slowly and locally. Davenport is not content with his first picture of the scene in his first paragraph. Here, he deepens it in his second, turning the experience in his hand, teasing out its underlying emotion, looking at it from different angles. An object seen once can be sharply defined. Seen twice, it loses its angularity and becomes more rounded. Seen three times, it takes on a fullness of dimension that gives it body and life.

A similar drive to look at something again and again can be seen in Davenport's essay. The more he sees, the more he lays the ground for what he feels and thinks about it. In the third paragraph, he tells us of the pride he feels in his small finds, a tiny arrowhead in blue flint, some small, shaped stones. By his fourth paragraph, he manages to tease out a complete thought:

Childhood is spent without introspection, in unreflective innocence. Adolescence turns its back on childhood in contempt and sometimes shame. We find our childhood later, and what we find in it is full of astounding surprises.

The thought is full-bodied, but incomplete. The essay form is only partly about evolving a thought. It matters how you get there as you go along. Thought takes on body in the essay, and though Davenport begins certain childhood reflections, as above, before he tells us just what those "surprises" are, he lets go of the idea and returns to the scenes in the upper Savannah Valley where he went as a boy to find arrowheads.

"Finding" is not really about finding a passion or even a hobby. It is about finding the life of a family and the center of what keeps it together. What they find is not so much arrows but themselves:

If I am grateful for the unintentional education of having been taught how to find things (all I have ever done, I think, with texts and pictures), I am even more grateful, in an inconsequential way, for my father's most astounding gift of all: being put at the throttle of a locomotive one night and allowed to drive it down the track for a whole five minutes. I loved trains, and grew up with them.

The phrase, "unintentional education," is a perfect expression of the underlying theme of any good admissions essay. "Unintentional" means not done on purpose. It actually covers a great range of purposelessness, from unhappily random and accidental all the way to happily fortuitous and serendipitous. For any young person, a great deal of life amounts to unintentional education. Teasing out the meaning in the real events of one's life, unpredictable as they often are, gives an admissions essay a sense of surprise. The writer of the essay at the mine starts to be surprised by events he sees unfolding there. The other writer is surprised by cutting an orange. Simple acts that are far-reaching in the rich assortment of tendencies they allow the writer to see in a developing self.

The object of an early, unintentional education does not have to be directed to a set academic goal. It is seeing itself:

I know that my sense of place, of occasion, even of doing anything at all, was shaped by those afternoons. It took me a while to realize that people can grow up without being taught how to see, to search surfaces for all the details, to check out a whole landscape for what it has to offer. My father became so good at spotting arrowheads that on roads with likely gullies he would find them from the car. Or give a commentary on what we might pick up were we to stop: "A nice spearhead back there by a maypop, but with the tip broken off."

Davenport can *see*. He does not claim much more than that for himself, but his essay is full of good seeing and we come to trust him as a good observer of things. The reader experiences a gradual growth of trust in Davenport's ability to learn from what he sees. A reader feels that he or she comes to inhabit a reality rather than a restricted idea of it. The reality may be quite hard to summarize (realities frequently are!) but the feeling that it is real lingers. In the end, the reader increasingly comes to feel that, somehow, in some organic way, Guy Davenport *is* in this essay. *The essay as a whole is its writer.*

This is exactly the feeling that an admissions essay should communicate to a college admissions committee. A reader of a personal essay should come to feel its genuineness and personalness, should come to some sense of the real presence of the writer. "Real presence" can sound almost magical, and there is indeed a kind of magic to feeling that the writer is with us as we read. But magic, even the magic of presence, is always carefully crafted. Guy Davenport seems to be with us at the end of the essay because he knows how to make himself appear to be with us. This appearance is anything but a trick. Davenport himself uses very little rhetoric or figurative language. The reality of his presence can be traced, not to a vague suggestiveness, but to a concreteness of observation that precedes thought and always accompanies it once formed. His prose never evaporates into ungrounded abstraction. It has a simple, direct humanity that proceeds from his senses. For when I speak of seeing, I mean not just the sense of sight but the full range of human sensory perception. Davenport keeps us anchored in the real by means of all five senses. We see him seeing arrowheads, but we also see him touching them, hear him talking about them, and sometimes even sense him smelling the places in which he finds them. His essay has a fullness of life because it shows a life seen fully, in all its incompletion:

And I learned from a whole childhood of looking in fields how the purpose of things ought perhaps to remain invisible, no more than half known. People who know exactly what they are doing seem to me to miss the vital part of any doing. My family, praises be unto the gods, never inspected anything that we enjoyed doing; criticism was strictly for universities, and not very much for them. Consequently I spent my childhood drawing, building things, writing, reading, playing, dreaming out loud, without the least comment from anybody. I learned later that I was thought not quite bright, for the patterns I discovered for myself were not quite things with nearby models. When I went off to college it was

with no purpose whatsoever: no calling in view, no pro-
fession, no ambition.

My students often do not know what to do with Davenport's essay at first. They are used to presenting their own highly directed ambitions and being praised for them. Davenport's undirected honesty both scares and intrigues them. He is honest, I tell them, because he owns his own experience, a step at a time, and because there has to be an increasing ownership of their own experience, a feeling that it involves a direct referent, before there can be an exactness in expressing it. Davenport himself makes it clear that each step of his finding was hard won. He does not relegate each of these stages to a distant past but shows each of them in their newness. So, when he expresses his ideas, they are often tentatively formulated, as though he knows he needs to hold them loosely, pending future experience. And throughout the essay, up to its final lines, he is aware that new experience comes crashing into his life, forcing him to search for new terms for new experiences. Here are the last three lines of the essay:

As we grew up, we began not to go on the expeditions. Not the last, but one of the last, afternoons found us toward sunset, findings in hand, ending up for the day with one of our rituals, a Coca-Cola from the icebox of a crossroads store. "They tell us over the radio," the pro-prietor said, "that a bunch of Japanese airplanes have blowed up the whole state of Hawaii."

The essay ends with the crashing intrusion of the outside world. Davenport does not go on to say how his little world changed, only that it did. The ending quite deliberately eschews omniscience. The writer may have worked hard to arrive at some small understanding of his own life, but there are still many things beyond it that can come at him from external sources. A reader has the sense that Davenport will now have to go on to experience a new kind of finding, while also having the feeling that, knowing him now a little, he will be ready for it. By the end, the richness of his title becomes clear. Finding is seeing, the finding of the arrowheads in the ground. Finding is feeling, his recovery of the binding force of family. And finding is thought, his idea that having learned to find things well, he will go on to find other things, equally rich in meaning for him.

~~~~~~~~~

Being clear in an admissions essay does not necessarily mean being clear about your plans. It means being clear about who you *are*. All students have plans. Plans change. Prospective future plans always have a vague edge around them, and in ending with what you plan to do you are not necessarily ending with *you*. A conclusion is a chance to leave a final sense of you with your reader. You want that impression to be specific rather than general. A story, a memory, or a detail about something have a much better chance of lodging in the mind of your reader than a general statement about your ambitions. Ambitions have a way of sounding alike. *I want to be a lawyer, a doctor, an accountant.* The field of knowledge at a college university is much broader than the limited number of such statements.

A tendency is always prospective. This holds particularly true for the admissions essay, which should end *tentatively.* Concluding, it opens up a wider field of possibility. (You may look ahead to pages 105–6 and 110–11 to see several possible endings to the mining essay.) Any essay is necessarily a short exercise. An admissions essay adopts an even narrower field of vision, building on close observation and tilting at last toward a particular interest, which may or may not, at this stage, point to a particular discipline. A good admissions essay leads into the writer's experiencing of unknown aspects of himself or herself. In this it is curious and venturesome, ending not with a sense of fixity of aim, but of *aim-in-process.* Davenport's essay ends with no sense of how he will move forward, just that he will. In having read him, the reader feels a cumulative confidence in his judgment, even if that judgment is at times uncertain and perhaps tinged with fear at the prospect of war. We end with a feeling that he is free to move in any direction, and because we have come to trust him, this sense of uncertainty is vested with a sense of wonder. The world may be uncertain, but the writer is open to it. His openness to inner and outer experience has given him a basic place in the world; a place to start from; a place from which it is possible to see, to feel, and to think, not to flinch.

The phrase "the essay as a whole" has about it a sense of unity like a circle. But a good essay is linear, and this chapter could just as easily be called "the essay as a line." An experience, accurately seen and felt, leads to a small epiphany, which in turn becomes an object of contemplation for the writer. One writer cuts an orange. Another goes to a mine. Both essays begin with some fixed state of understanding that breaks open under the pressure of experience. Far from proceeding from a set of postulates—"I want to become a geologist"—the essay shows an experience in all its fluidity. So many markers of college admissions are interested in the chimera of invariant elements of personality, such as the unchanging aspects of math or verbal ability, represented in a single number or series of numbers. But the admissions essay can take in the possibility of *change*. How does a new interest or awareness develop? What conditions favored it? And most important of all, what is the process by which such change occurs?

Here, it is important to remember how much objective research at the university deals with process. Literary critics study the process of reading. Law professors look at the ongoing processes by which laws are interpreted and reinterpreted. Scientific research studies the division of a cell, the breakdown of a protein, the splitting of an atom. Each tries to make a fresh attempt to understand the way in which change takes place. Each tries to be sensitive to the *event* in and of itself, moving away from simple abstractions which would describe it. The model of academic research is always the low-level inference, the smallest, rather than the largest, idea that can be derived from an event or experience. In this way, knowledge is advanced, one perception at a time. The point reached is not a point on a line but a moving point in space that may be crossed, at any time, by any number of lines. The situation may be confusing, but what matters here is holding off on approximations until the dust settles on knowledge. Davenport's title is exemplary here. It is "Finding," not "Found."

~~~~~~~~

Not knowing is part of writing. Or more accurately: not knowing, knowing, and wanting to know are bound up together in the act of writing. They have to be. Writing without knowing leads to groundless speculation. Writing and knowing can lead to overconfidence. And writing and wanting to know can lead to very partial and incomplete knowledge. No writer knows fully what the next sentence is going to be, though often they have an approximate idea. Thought needs room to drift through seeing and feeling before it becomes thought.

This too goes for your plans. Being clear about them does not mean being conclusive. It means being as clear as you can. It means, in all the senses that Davenport uses the word, "finding."

6

The Master Narrative

MOST COLLEGE applications are written in bits and pieces. The essay, being longer, tends to be written first. The shorter questions follow, taken by most students as something to be filled in at the last minute. They tend to be seen as completely separate questions, a bit like numbered questions on a final exam. A sense of the whole is utterly lacking. Only occasionally does a student bring a feeling of connection to the questions and answers, but even then, it does not go very far. I have found that most students remember their scores on the SAT for years, but hardly any can remember a word they said about themselves on their college applications. Having invested so little of themselves in the experience, they often have no memory of representing themselves in any meaningful way.

Many admit to having been preoccupied with answering the questions exactly as asked. In high schools, they are used to being penalized for not answering the question. There, they develop the habit of reading questions largely in black and white terms. They come to a question thinking that someone, somewhere, has a fixed, perfect answer to it in mind, and they feel they have no choice but to find, somehow or other, the *right* answer. A lot of my students are very surprised when I tell them that many readers on admissions committees have little awareness of exactly which question the student is answering. They tend to skip from answer to answer, perusing them, trying to get a sense of the student. The applications themselves may not be read in any particular order. Different readers might begin with the essay, scores, grades, supplements, or letters. Many readers often browse an application before looking at it in greater detail. In this way, the success of a college application is largely literary. That is, admissions officers respond not to any demonstrable logic or idea but to a certain felt intensity of patterning *among the answers*. The pattern need not be complex. What matters is that there is one. Our minds can adhere to parts of many things at once. We can be put through somewhat of a stretch among the parts so long as we sense there is an integrity among the things themselves. In a college application, this integrity, this sense of the whole, is what I call the application's *master narrative*.

A master narrative calls for a high degree of design in each part. But a very particular kind of design. A good master narrative would have a clear voice, a good central story, and a series of related stories. The voice is the basis for a story, the story for related stories, but a clear voicing of self *throughout* a narrative is what holds things together. By now the idea of voice should be familiar, but as we shall see, it takes on new meaning in this extended context of *story*.

~~~~~~~~~~

Words, sentences, and paragraphs are part of the whole of an admissions essay, but even taken together, they are not yet the whole. An essay can be very well argued without really being alive. This recognition goes to the heart of the admissions essay. It may make an argument for you, but the means by which it best does so are not argumentative. It has to *show* you seeing, feeling, and thinking. The means by which it does this are less the ordinary means of logical argument, than the more extraordinary means of storytelling. We have already seen that you need to represent yourself in as close to three dimensions as possible in the admissions essay. A good argumentative essay can produce a strong but limited impression, a bit like a closing argument in a legal case. But taken on its own, it falls short of fullness. Arguments can often fall into clear and established channels of thought where you wind up repeating things many others have already said. These things may be essential pieces of an argument, but overall, they lack a sense of *you*, of your inner life and being, and they often fail to provide fresh terms for new feelings. In this context, it is better to tell a story about yourself than to make an argument. In telling a story, all the elements of your experience become available to your awareness, and your prose becomes real and effective in demonstrating who you are.

My students tend to do best with small, intense experiences that allow them, in a circumscribed context, to begin to find a genuineness in writing. In this way, there can begin to be that close matching of observation, feeling, and thought that we have seen is conducive to good prose.

These small experiences must be at such a scale that they can begin to be probed for an inward direction. They often involve feelings at their most private. Our writer in West Virginia is unlikely to have shared any hesitations about the protest at the mine. He or she may feel isolated or even hopeless about ever beginning to say what has actually been seen and felt. The writer may even be unaware of the full measure of what has been seen and felt, save for an uneasy feeling that the distance between the writer and the group has grown increasingly great. The writer has the feeling of not quite belonging there anymore and is often not sure why. Here is where starting small counts. Seeing the trembling of a man's hand was a breakthrough for this writer. It started to change the writer's view of the man, overcoming the malignancy of an initial perception of him. By sharpening what is seen, feelings about it can also begin to be sharpened as well. The trembling of the man's hand did not quite seem to belong to the scene as expected to unfold. The truth is that it takes time for a writer to see real experience as a solid basis for writing, to begin to see what they see freshly, instead of seeing what they think *should* be seen.

This is where the short story comes in. The short story is a highly evolved literary form for narrating short, intense experiences. An admissions essay is best seen as a story with an argumentative turn at the end. It uses story to build to a climax, then draws a meaning from the story. Everything in the essay should be integral to its development. The story helps the reader to get to know you and leads them to the point where you have decided to seek admission to college. But the story is crucial not because it leads to that point but because it establishes you as a person. A reader comes to know and trust your voice. This trust, established in the grain of the story, is then carried over to the case you make from it about going to college. The case is not the moral of the story but its denouement, its natural conclusion.

A good story has a quality of motion, of flow, of variety. At its best, it shows experience being modified by each living event. Stories have a clear edge of immediacy. A story can show someone experiencing something *completely*. The form revolves around what James Joyce called an epiphany, or a discovery about something previously unknown in a life that is very basic to it. This discovery is often an all-out moment of self-awareness because now a pattern, an underlying order, has been seen in experience, though often without the means to comfortably integrate it into life. In this way, the short story is a very discomfiting form. It strips a mask off experience, taking away its preconceived forms. It leads the reader to see the evidence of a new situation, as it is, rather than distorting it to fit a pattern which it already holds.

~~~~~~~~~

One of my favorite short stories is "The Use of Force" by William Carlos Williams. It is two or three pages long, about the length of an admissions essay. The story takes place in about the time it takes to read it. Williams was a doctor as well as a poet, and he often treated poor patients with diphtheria—the subject of this story. Not much is told as background, though much is shown and even more is implied at the edges. Here is the beginning:

They were new patients to me, all I had was the name, Olson. Please come down as soon as you can; my daughter is very sick.

When I arrived I was met by the mother, a big startled looking woman, very clean and apologetic who merely said, Is this the doctor? and let me in. In the back, she added. You must excuse us, doctor, we have her in the kitchen where it is warm. It is very damp here sometimes.

The story begins with good seeing. The first paragraph sets a tone of urgency. The second shows the mother, "a big startled looking woman." The word "startled" stands out and sets the tone of the story and foresees its action. It means both agitated by surprise or alarm or to cause to start involuntarily, as from a sudden shock. Williams never actually says the family is poor. He shows them in poverty by having the mother invite him into the house's only warm room. Then we meet the sick daughter:

The child was fully dressed and sitting on her father's lap near the kitchen table. He tried to get up, but I motioned for him not to bother, took off my overcoat and started to look things over. I could see that they were all very nervous, eyeing me up and down distrustfully. As often, in such cases, they weren't telling me more than they had to, it was up to me to tell them; that's why they were spending three dollars on me.

Emotion now comes more forcefully into play. The family is nervous and suspicious. The doctor decides to take a throat culture and the girl fights back, screaming. Her parents try to hold her down. Emotion floods the room. In quick succession Williams writes of embarrassment, apprehension, shame, and finally hysteria. While the parents hold down the girl, Williams forces himself on her:

The child's mouth was already bleeding. Her tongue was cut and she was screaming in wild hysterical shrieks.

Perhaps I should have desisted and come back in an hour or more. No doubt it would have been better. But I have seen at least two children lying dead in bed of neglect in such cases, and feeling that I must get a diagnosis now or never I went at it again. But the worst of it was that I too had got beyond reason. I could have torn the child apart in my own fury and enjoyed it. It was a pleasure to attack her. My face was burning with it.

The damned little brat must be protected against her own idiocy, one says to one's self at such times. Others must be protected against her. It is social necessity. And all these things are true. But a blind fury, a feeling of adult shame, bred of a longing for muscular release are the operatives. One goes on to the end.

In a final unreasoning assault I overpowered the child's neck and jaws. I forced the heavy silver spoon back of her teeth and down her throat till she gagged. And there it was – both tonsils covered with membrane. She had fought valiantly to keep me from knowing her secret. She had been hiding that sore throat for three days at least and lying to her parents in order to escape just such an outcome as this.

Seeing leads to feeling leads to thinking—not separately, but bound up together in one terrible moment. Seeing her symptoms, wading his way through her resistance, Williams reasons his way to an unreasoning attack on her. He means to help her but the force he uses takes on, in itself, its own unreasoning impetus. The power of the story resides in the inseparability of observation and emotion and thought. The doctor, at first only an observer, is drawn into the emotion of the situation and sees himself changed by it. Feeling leads to thinking, but the thought is tainted by the feeling and becomes "unreasoning." The truth of his story resides in its fusion of clinical observation, strong emotion, and reactive thought. As Williams says beautifully, "all these things are true."

It would be wrong to expect a good story to conclude more than this. Williams is careful to hold back more commentary than is implied by his title, "The Use of Force." Like many short stories, it contains a thought that is *almost* reached. Stories are suggestive because they always seem to be on the verge of saying something declarative. But they often stop just short, as here, where Williams' fatalistic "[o]ne goes on to the end" captures his needing to overpower the girl. It is just enough to raise the question of the use of force in the mind of the reader, and in this sense, the story offers not the completion of a thought but the beginning of one. It starts something that it does not end.

A good story can be very useful in opening an admissions essay. It shows an openness to experience and an ability to register it without twisting it to fit some preconceived structure. It shows a writer able to take in the evidence of a complex situation, showing it as it is without forcing closure on it. And it favors an honesty of articulation that allows Williams to say something like "one goes on in the end," a grim statement, but an honest one. In this way, a story can be good data as well as good literature. They are case studies. Psychologists collect stories because these case studies allow them to show psychological states in their irreducible complexity. Historians collect stories as oral histories. Williams's story itself is often anthologized for reading by doctors. Many of my students wanting to go into medicine have volunteered at hospitals, and many, reading this, have reported similar experiences. Reading Williams's story both helped them validate their own experience and allowed them to look closely at the means Williams used to represent his experience. Most, of course, were not able to write a story as good as this. But they were able to find and write a story that was *good enough* for the purposes of a college application. By this I mean a high degree of competence that can normally be achieved by a certain care in storytelling using plain language, short sentences, and clear-edged details. It need not have the special density of literature, just the clarity, directness, and intensity for which Williams's story is a good model.

The story itself, of course, draws no conclusion other than the words of its title, "The Use of Force." An admission essay based on this experience would have to go further in pressing the issue of the use of force, though in a way that did justice to the nuance of the story itself. It opens the question of the degree of reason involved in the use of force once force begins to be applied. This holds true for almost any difficult situation or problem.

An underlying reality is always present. This reality can be addressed in the central story, told in the main personal essay, or in a short answer to one of the supplemental questions. Answers to other questions would be linked to it, cementing a reader's memory of the central binding narrative of the application. The reminders need not be large. But each supplemental question, as answered, should reverberate with the application's most powerful story.

Our writer at the mine might approach the reality of mining in one register:

Back home after one of these trips to West Virginia, I turned on the air conditioner full-blast. I closed my eyes, thinking, I'm glad I'm not there. Then I opened them with a start. I was there. That air conditioner was blowing coal dust at me as sure as it was at those miners, because here in Pennsylvania a lot of our energy comes from coal. They forced it out of the earth every day, shortening their lives so I could stretch out in my parents' living room in Montgomery County under a cool metallic wind. It reminded me yet again how bound up we were in the energy we consumed. I opened one of the books on low-carbon housing I showed in my table at a school fair. It listed a number of factors for installing a window in a low-carbon house:

$$U_{w, installed} = \frac{(U_{glass} \times A_{glass}) + (U_{frame} \times A_{frame}) + (\psi_{spacer} \times L_{glass}) + (\psi_{installation} \times U_{installation})}{A_{window}}$$

All of this for installing a window! Leading a low-carbon life was going to be anything but easy, and I saw that it would take a lot of study before I had even the beginning of a real idea what to do about it. I know now that I am ready to begin.

Our prospective geologist might approach the reality of geology in another register:

Last summer I took a course in field geology at the University of Georgia. They have a great site near Stone Mountain. Six or eight of my classmates were dangling from a cliff, chipping off rocks in the ninety-degree heat. I was on the ground below, minding the ropes. A trailer pulled up on the road behind me. A woman got out with her two teenagers. Pointing up, she said,

"Now I want you to see what will happen to you if you don't do good in school. You'll wind up like them, roped together, hacking at rocks for the rest of your life. They're being punished for what they did."

Hacking at rocks! The students in the class laughed at the story. The teachers didn't. I asked one of them why. He then said something I'll never forget.

"She's right. We're taking things from the earth. It looks harmless when you're just taking specimens, but we're just the advance scouts for a big invasion. A few years back I worked as an exploration geologist in Mongolia, looking for gold. Our job was to find it, not tell anyone, then get out of there fast so companies could buy

up the land before anyone knew. We betrayed every sin-
gle person who helped us. Sometimes I can't sleep. I think
exploration geology's right up there in ethics with bail
bonds and ready-mix concrete. And petroleum geology
is not much better."

I have no answer for this. My teacher didn't either,
even after a long career. Our well-being depends on the
minerals we extract from the earth—at almost any cost.
I made up my mind to go forward with geology, but with
eyes wide open. A science is all that it knows, but it is
also all that it does.

Every short answer should lead to a long answer. Every
parallel narrative in a master narrative must have the
effect of underscoring the main narrative and making it more memorable. It gently redirects the reader's
attention back to the key elements in the story, instead
of moving the reader off away from them. Many unexpected things can be folded into the narrative in this
reverberative way. An applicant who is an accomplished
musician can be shown organizing concerts for very sick
patients who cannot leave the hospital. An athletically
inclined student could organize sports demonstrations.
The stories told at the outer orbits of the master narrative do not even have to be academic. They need only
contribute in some way to the overall integration of the
master narrative's picture of an applicant open to experience in socially constructive ways.

It is no easy thing to coordinate stories. Most people can tell a simple story with a single thread. A story with a single thread is a short story. Most students can readily write a serviceable one. But a master narrative relies on something like a novel's ability to bring together a number of separate but related stories under a central frame. But only a very small number. Most novels are a braid of two to three stories.

Too many stories confuse the listener and make it too hard to find a commonality in them. The stories must appear to be close but not too close, far but not too far. The art here is that of *mutuality*. A mutual world is a shared world with clear boundaries. A novel like *War and Peace* has two complete sets of characters, but most of them live in a fairly small social world. The sense of three dimensions in narrative comes from the intertwining of stories in a clear and restricted context. For a master narrative to come to life, it must take in a number of different stories that have an inner relationship to one another. The stories must be related but not identical. Time and place are usually sufficient as binders. The sense of a common time holds together the various short stories in Ernest Hemingway's *In Our Time*. The sense of a common place holds together the stories in Sandra Cisneros's *The House on Mango Street*. These books are good models because they do not over-coordinate their stories. The stories are there for their vividness and their genuineness. Chosen on these grounds, they live together very well.

In Our Time has some long short stores interleaved by many shorter ones, some as short as a paragraph. The longer stories show one character, Nick Adams, in many situations—on a camping trip, in the trenches, at a bullfight in Spain. This one character anchors the book. These stories mostly take place in isolated rural places, a railroad line in the woods, a cabin in upstate Michigan, an old lumbering town. These stories set a certain tone of insularity and muted violence, showing drunkenness, fights, hunting, and fishing. But between them are some very short stories, most not longer than a paragraph, set in italics. This is the first of them:

Everybody was drunk. The whole battery was drunk going along the road in the dark. We were going to the Champagne. The lieutenant kept riding his horse out into the fields and saying to him, "I'm drunk, I tell you, mon vieux. Oh, I am so soused." We went along the road all night in the dark and the adjutant kept riding up alongside my kitchen and saying, "You must put it out. It is dangerous. It will be observed." We were fifty kilometers from the front but the adjutant worried about the fire in my kitchen. It was funny going along the road. That was when I was a kitchen corporal.

It is up to the reader to see that this is Nick Adams. These small short stories are hard, sharp, and violent. They make the implicit violence of the longer stories explicit. The reader does not learn until the sixth italicized story, which begins *"Nick sat against the wall of the church,"* that this is Nick. But by then the reader has put it together. Hemingway counts on this, and you can too. A series of stories creates an implicit line of affiliation. When Nick goes to war, his experience is pockmarked by what he sees in the trenches of the First World War.

Experiences come at him faster than explanations for them. Repeated sharp shards of story show him embedded in a real world far from the one he was raised in. College applications, too, should show the writer going out into the world. These forays, like Nick's, can be short, vivid, and often unresolved. Here, the writer recruits the reader to help make up the story. It might seem that this is too much of an act of faith on the writer's part, but readers love unresolved stories. Putting small stories in your application recruits the reader to help make up your stories.

Following Hemingway, our writer at the mine might offer this sharply observed vignette of a miner:

The miner wasn't dirty. I expected his face to blackened with soot, blinking at me though the coal dust caught in his eyes. He wore clean, trim jeans and a new chambray work shirt. A shiny lunch box in one hand, he walked along a tidy path between the outbuildings of the mine. Seeing me notice him, the representative of the mine came up to me and started to talk, almost talking over my thoughts.

*"We have locker rooms now. They wash up. See? It's
not so bad. This is a modern mine. I can't take you down
there just now—regulations you know—but I promise
you it's a clean and well-lighted place. I'll have to look
for some pictures."*

Hemingway is a master of understatement. He relies on
the reader to infer his meaning. Here, inference actually strengthens the meaning of the passage in a college
application. The representative may or may not be con-
cealing something, but the writer knows he or she is at a
coal mine and that coal mines are dirty. So, something is
definitely wrong here. In a college application, a writer
might add a few sentences that give a hint of a direction
in college:

*Was this true? How could I find out it wasn't? He was
not about to let me in. I saw now I was in the position
of a real journalist, seeing something real, something
important, and not knowing what it was, but needing
to find out.*

Another good model for interrelating stories is Sandra Cisneros's *The House on Mango Street*. Most of the
stories move in and out of the experience of Esperanza
Cordero, who grows up in a poor neighborhood in Chi-
cago. Many pivot around characters who are trying to
get out of the neighborhood. The seeing and feeling of
their plight is beautifully rendered in "Linoleum Roses":

Sally got married like we knew she would, young and not ready but married just the same. She met a marshmallow salesman at a school bazaar, and she married him in another state where it's legal to get married before eighth grade. She has her husband and her house now, her pillowcases and her plates. She says she is in love, but I think she did it to escape.

Sally says she likes being married because now she gets to buy her own things when her husband gives her money. She is happy, except sometimes her husband gets angry and once he broke the door where his foot went through, though most days he is okay. Except he won't let her talk on the telephone. And he doesn't let her look out the window. And he doesn't like her friends, so nobody gets to visit her unless he is working.

She sits at home because she is afraid to go outside without his permission. She looks at all the things they own: the towels and the toaster, the alarm clock and the drapes. She likes looking at the walls, at how neatly their corners meet, the linoleum roses on the floor, the ceiling smooth as wedding cake.

The thought behind the story comes a little later in the book, in a story called "A House of My Own":

Not a flat. Not an apartment in back. Not a man's house. Not a daddy's. A house all my own. With my porch and my pillow, my pretty purple petunias. My books and my stories. My two shoes waiting beside the bed.

Nobody to shake a stick at.

Nobody's garbage to pick up after.

Only a house quiet as snow, a space for myself to go,
clean as paper before the poem.

In Cisneros's book, the seeing and feeling and thinking of the neighborhood, as a *place*, is splayed out across many small stories. The titles of the stories include things closely observed ("House," "Hairs," "Red Clowns," "Linoleum Roses," "The Family of Little Feet"), things vividly felt ("Laughter," "Hips," "Born Bad," "Beautiful and Cruel"), and things that draw out the underlying thoughts ("A House of My Own," "Mango Says Goodbye Sometimes"). Cisneros approaches the unity of seeing and feeling and thinking from every angle. The first story, "The House on Mango Street," is the set piece of her master narrative. It tells us about Esperanza's house, her street, her feelings about it, and ends with her plans: "I knew then I had to have a house. A real house. One I could point to. But this isn't it."

The intensity of place in *The House on Mango Street* is carefully conveyed by a selection of close observations invested with feeling. There are no clinically observed details in Cisneros's book. Seeing always comes fully vested with feeling:

But the house on Mango Street is not the way they told it at all. It's small and red with tight steps in front and windows so small you'd think they were holding their breath. Bricks are crumbling in places, and the front door is so swollen you have to push hard to get in. There

113

is no front yard, only four little elms the city planted by the curb. Out back is a small garage for the small car we don't own yet, and a small yard that looks smaller between the two buildings on either side. There are stairs in our house, but they're ordinary hallway stairs, and the house has only one washroom.

Cisneros begins, as writers often have to, by making it clear she is speaking as a corrective. The house has previously been seen poorly, if at all. She is *looking again* at what others have seen many times without seeing. Note how each act of seeing is immediately invested with a clear qualification of feeling. This happens in nearly every sentence. The house is "small and red" but "holding its breath." "Bricks are crumbling" and "the front door is swollen." And "[o]ut back is a small garage" for "the car we don't own yet." In each case, Cisneros adjusts what is seen to show what is felt. The house is not a perfect little house. It is airless, swollen, and filled with things they do not even own. The house here is not an object in a landscape but a very human portrait she takes care to invest with human attributes.

The effect is to deepen the seeing by layering it with feeling in an orderly way, carefully circling the house, seeing it in front, going around back, looking at the garage, then going inside. It is not often easy to put feelings into words, but basing a feeling, as she does, on a descriptive formulation anchors the feeling in a particular place and makes the feeling more easily communicable. It also gives the scene itself a sense of warmth. The experience of feeling thickens the description, vesting it with life.

Hemingway's book of stories moves from place to place, united by the experience of a single character. Cisneros's book moves from character to character, united by an experience of a single place. In both books, actions are described in terms close to their immediate experiencing. Both books show rather than tell. Each story acts as an addition to experience, making it hard to come to a set idea about anything because so many new experiences come at the reader, one after another. The effect can be a little confusing at times, but it is also satisfyingly real. New experiences *can* be threatening. Both Nick and Esperanza are very aware they are passing though troubled worlds. But they seem to do so without fear, because they see the world around them with such cumulative clarity.

This cumulative clarity is the aim of a master narrative. In a college application, the personal essay usually serves as the frame, setting the time and the place for the other stories. These other small stories are anything but peripheral. For a master narrative to come to life, it must summon up a number of different stories that have an inner relationship to one another. The principle is simple here: a theme with variations. In music, variation is a formal technique where a short, striking theme is repeated in an altered form. The central theme is usually a melody that is later varied in rhythm, harmony, or voicing. Once articulated, a theme can have very different ranges of variation. In Hemingway, the range is wide. In Cisneros, it is somewhat narrower. In both cases, these variations have their limits. You do not want your readers to strain in seeing the connections between the stories you tell. The mining essay should not veer into talking about drilling for oil. The geology essay should keep to geology. It should not deal with chemistry, unless it is geochemistry, or physics, unless it is geophysics. In this, the personal essay serves as the frame, setting the time and the place for the other stories. For a master narrative to come to life, it must take in a number of different stories that have an inner relationship to one another. A good master narrative may be larger in scope than a single narrative, but it should always carry your reader back into the heart of your application. *In Our Time* and *The House on Mango Street* are both good models here because both deal with characters who leave small worlds and enter larger ones—very much the situation of an applicant going to college.

~~~~~~~~~~

A master narrative is not a master explanation. If the story leads too easily to a moral, it is a fable, not a story. Ernest Hemingway once said, "If you're looking for messages, try Western Union." This goes, too, for most of the easily sent messages found in the personal essay. Many are very familiar fill-in-the-blank topics. *Overcoming X to do Y. The first X to do Y. The youngest X to do Y.* These topics are only useable if you can find something to say within them that is uniquely your own. Using a set topic has another danger, too. It can lead you to perceiving things in preconceived categories, forcing closure in the form of clichés. There is an unmistakable sadness about choosing to write in a voice that is only trying to say things in exactly the same way that others have said them. Writing only begins to succeed when writers themselves determine the reality from which they are writing. At first, you may not be able to fit what you are seeing into your preconceptions of it. Writing an essay that is genuinely your own involves a newness of perception, a finding of the shape of the experience in the act of living it. By a master narrative, I do not mean a closed system with a rigid beginning, middle, and end into which your experience is forced. I mean a narrative with an easy and loose conjoining of its parts in which your knowledge has a quality of immediacy to it, a quality of being modified by each new understanding you add to the sum of your understandings. It takes time to develop a basic trust in this process of narration, which allows you to begin representing your own inner experiencing of the world, which allows you to be seen for who you are, wherever you are.

7

Three Case Studies

T<small>HIS</small> <small>CHAPTER</small> looks at how I work with students. My own process is implicit in earlier chapters, where I show successive drafts of an essay getting better and better. But I am very aware that part of the reason they were getting better is that I was there. I played an analytic role in every phase. I asked questions, probed answers, and encouraged a certain amount of productive drift. My own method with students might be considered a kind of analysis for writing based on phenomenological principles. I encourage students to look closely at the world around them and to build their response to what they see and feel as carefully as they can.

This chapter consists of three short case studies. I call them "The Photographer," "The Skater," and "The Marine Biologist." Each goes to a groundedness in seeing, feeling, and thinking. All three forces exist in each of the essays, but each writer gives them a different inflection. In each of the essays, the developmental impetus is different. "The Photographer" grounds an essay in seeing. Feeling and thought follow, but the essay is primarily a thing seen. "The Skater" grounds an essay in reverberative feeling. The feeling is led to by good seeing, and clear thought follows, but the emotion of "The Skater" runs over in both directions, tinting seeing and tempering thought. "The Marine Biologist" grounds an essay in thought; in this case, a scientific problem. Seeing and feeling are there, but they primarily act as the proving ground for thought. The need for this resides in the problem being reconsidered as new things are seen and dictates the emphasis, which, even though a little abstract at times, is as natural to this writer as seeing and feeling are to the others.

I worked with each student for about six months. I met with each of them for one hour a week until the last month before the deadline, when we met for two hours a week. The work fell into three distinct phases, given below. In each phase, the essence of my method is that I never left the student's text for very long. The text, with its emerging voice, is the source from which all development issues.

The first phase is to show what has been written. I ask each student to give me a complete portfolio of writing going back two or three years. I then choose a piece I consider typical of the student's style, or if there is a draft of the admissions essay, I use that. I go over the choice and meaning of every word, the grammar and inflection of every sentence, and the structure and organization of every paragraph. Normally I mark up the piece at great length. I often ask students to rewrite individual sentences but never whole essays at this point. If they start to struggle, I sometimes write good sentences that might work in that context, taking care to give them four or five different options for proceeding. Each sentence leads in a very different direction and results in a very different essay. These sentences are meant only to show the way. Students never use anything I write in their own applications.

The second phase is to show other possibilities for writing. These can be highly variable. I show them parts of books, complete essays, even fragments. The range can be seen in what I quote in this book. There are selections from a chapter in *The Road to Wigan Pier*; complete essays, such as those by Guy Davenport and Elizabeth Bishop; and short fragments by a range of other writers. Sometimes I ask a student to read a whole book, but only if we have time. The books that turn out to be the most influential may surprise the reader. Two are from the nineteenth century and the third was written in the 1950s. At this point, I begin to explain how writing depends, in the first instance, on clear perception resulting from close observation, accurately observed emotion, and tentative (but tangible) motions of thought, supported in each instance by the clear examples of earlier writers. These examples come from books I happened to know. Often students introduce me to others.

The third phase amounts to a break in style. The way a student writes changes. This change can register in so many ways that I hesitate to characterize it in short form. The breaking of style, as the word implies, is often sudden and uneven. A student starts to see a new way of writing before he or she is fully able to inhabit it. Sometimes a student's style changes before the deadline of the application; sometimes it doesn't. Some students have a better ear for language than others. Students who have a musical ear for language often seem to move along faster. But the goal of a clear, plain voice is almost always attainable by anyone.

This scheme of three phases is only a very general scheme of organization. The interest in these narratives comes from what the student presented me with and what we were able to do during our time together. The development took place only in and around writing. The essence of my method is that I never leave the text. Its basis is an attentive reader paying attention to an inattentive writer. I often hear, "What I *meant* was—" And I find I have to say, "but what you *said* was—" It takes time for a student to learn that meaning to say something is not the same as saying it. A writer has to have a reasonable degree of confidence about how a reader will read what has been written on the page. In practical terms, someone needs to point out to them what they have *actually* said, right *there* on the page, parsing the words they have actually chosen. This is mostly what I do below, and my ongoing commentary forms the basis of my process. It is often an education in itself for my students to see me trying to construe their writing, struggling with their imprecision. Young writers have little sense that they are being read, that there is a real person on the other end trying to put together some kind of picture from what they have written. Even the idea of their intention, which they often suppose is clear, comes into focus. After looking closely at their prose, many are often very likely to conclude that their intention is very far from clear to them. More often than not, they come to see that they, in fact, have a different intention and that they have to start all over again.

These case studies differ in several respects from the two essays analyzed so far, the ones about the mine and the orange. Those are representative composites. They cull all the features of strong and weak essays into two clear examples, or to use the more precise Latin term, *exempla*. I have taken care in composing them to make sure that every feature of both essays comes out of a particular strength or weakness I have observed in an individual student essay over the years. But the themes of the essays, and the construction of the underlying individuals, are my own. This goes to a policy central to my practice. My work with students is private. I do not advertise or solicit testimonials. My students are free to comment on our work, but only if they choose to do so. In presenting these studies, I have taken great care to change any identifying markers. Person, place, time, and situation are all different. Here, I have been guided by the example of clinical psychologists, who in published narratives alter all details—except for the crux of them—to protect the identities of their patients. Behind the screen of these three case studies stand three discrete individuals. I have tried to render enough of them to give a full picture. But I am also very aware that the picture is a representation I have carefully devised in letter, though I have done my best to make it accurate in spirit. The spirit can be found in the morphology of development in each case. *Who* the student is may be screened, but *how* and *why* they develop as they do is placed under continuous scrutiny. In this way, I hope these three studies will add a further dimension of the real to this book, though admittedly, at one necessary remove.

These studies should be useful for tutors. But they will be just as useful for students, who, I have found, need to internalize this process to become good editors of their own prose. My students are always asking me how other students have done in the past. Here is part of the answer.

~~~~~~~~~~

My first case was a student who had no academic interests. She wanted to go to college; that was all. She did what she was told to do in school, and she had good grades. Her palette of activities was colorless—clubs she joined, she explained to me, mostly because her friends joined them, too. Her father was in finance. She had moved a lot during her childhood, often in the middle of the school year. She was often bored in class. She said her mind wandered a lot.

I did not ask much about the schools. She had been in too many of them. Very little from them had taken hold. Her affiliation with subjects was also thin. But again and again, she came back to saying how she drifted a lot, thinking about things.

"What kind of things?"

"Well, images."

"What kind of images?"

"I don't know. I just kind of like taking pictures."

Shyly, she took out her iPhone and started showing me pictures. For years, she had gone around cities taking pictures of things. She had lived in different cities—Brussels, Hong Kong, London—before coming to Philadelphia. I saw pictures of the Bourse in Amsterdam, the HSBC Bank building in Hong Kong, the Houses of Parliament in London, and Independence Hall and the Liberty Bell in Philadelphia. The pictures were mostly middle-distance shots of buildings, composed like postcards.

"But those aren't my favorites," she confided. "You know, I'm a sort of a closet nature photographer."

She had been to Glacier National Park the summer before, and started to show me those photographs. Right away I sensed a difference. The photographs seemed highly composed. In one was a meadow with a small cabin off to one side and complex clouds above, taken in the Flathead Valley in Montana. Another showed a braided stream, taken on the Little Big Horn River near the Custer Monument. The third showed a formally dressed man on a rock, looking out over the low fog covering Lake McDonald Valley on the west side of Glacier National Park.

Seeing these, I quickly used my computer to bring up images of *The Hay Wain* (1821) by John Constable, *The Oxbow* (1836) by Thomas Cole, and *Wanderer Above the Sea of Fog* (1818) by Casper David Friedrich—three common examples of early nineteenth-century romantic paintings of nature.

"So you were copying these?" I asked.

"Never seen them before," she said flatly.

"Really?"

"Really."

"Then where do you suppose they came from?"

She shook her head. She really had no idea.

So, I told her a story about when I started out writing. I wrote a description of a fog, fog everywhere, settling in over downtown Minneapolis late in November, slowly creeping through the warehouses, grain elevators, and freight yards north of Hennepin Avenue. Only many years later, I told her, did I find I was working from the famous opening paragraphs of Charles Dickens's *Bleak House* (1851):

Fog everywhere. Fog up the river, where it flows among green aits and meadows; fog down the river, where it rolls defiled among the tiers of shipping and the water- side pollutions of a great (and dirty) city. Fog on the Essex marshes, fog on the Kentish heights. Fog creeping into the cabooses of collier-brigs; fog lying out on the

*yards, and hovering in the rigging of great ships; fog
drooping on the gunwales of barges and small boats.*

"How do you suppose that was?" I asked her.

"Maybe you saw it somewhere."

"No. Never. Just like you. I didn't read it till I got to
Stanford."

I saw at that moment, for the first time in our work
together, she was genuinely interested in a problem.

She crossed her legs. "So you're telling me you don't
have to have read something to have read it."

"To be read by it," I said.

"So I wasn't seeing?" she asked.

"In a way, those images were seeing you. Or they
were seeing through you, without you having to have
seen them."

I was not sure where this was going. I saw how she
left shaking her head. But in our next session, she came
back with a dozen photographs, each carefully indexed
to a classic work of art. Among them were a picture
she took in Holland indexed to Vermeer's *View on Delft*
(1660–1661); a picture she took in the Midwest (she
couldn't remember where) linked to Rembrandt's etch-
ing *The Three Trees* (1643); and a picture she took of
some dry, grassy hills in southeastern Montana, upland
near the Crow Reservation, that reminded her of the
odd craggy landscape behind the *Mona Lisa* (1503).

"I found all these online," she said. "They seem to be
everywhere."

She was right about that. They did seem to be every-where. It was possible to see them without ever really registering that they had been seen, as though with peripheral vision. I told her there were even some theorists, like Carl Jung, who felt there was a collec-tive unconscious of images, but that I had my doubts, though I was quite sure that these images somehow cir-culated freely among human cultures. I told her, too, that the provenance of these images could be very diffi-cult to trace with any degree of certainty, though many had tried.

Soon she had a whole archive of images. Only then, after she started to be curious about where they all came from, did I give her some books to read. I gave her chapters from Roland Barthes' *Mythologies* (1957), E. H. Gombrich's *The History of Art* (1950), and Rudolf Arnheim's *Art and Visual Perception* (1954). These texts might at first glance seem too sophisticated for a high school student, but the problem she had stumbled on was itself sophisticated, so I felt she was ready for them.

I am never sure, when I give students books, which ones will take. I usually give them at least three at a time, hoping for a little range. She took something away from each of them. In Barthes, she started to see that an image could form part of a history of ideas. In Gom-brich, she found that any image could have an inner structure that was deeply historical. In Arnheim, she found that certain standing images informed our visual perception. Then she was ready to write. Suddenly she found she had a lot to say:

Images come from somewhere. They are all around us, and we often do not see them. Our cars pass a shifting array of them on the highway, and the images we see on television pass by so quickly that they almost seem to be a blur.

Reading this, I told her not to talk about the problem abstractly and categorically but to talk about how she realized the problem was a problem, speaking more distinctly in her own voice, using *I* rather than *we*. It was only as this point that I began to explain how good writing is a compound of seeing, feeling, and thinking. Next, she wrote:

The picture was one among many. I don't remember thinking about anything as I took it, just the passing thought that the scene looked like a picture. I did not stop and wonder why it looked like a picture, but I remember taking them quickly, aware that the scene that had composed itself before my eyes would pass very quickly, and be lost.

I was in the mountains of Montana. It was July in Glacier National Park. It took some effort to get high enough to really see anything, but when I got to the top of Mount Siyeh there was already someone there. He was not dressed like a hiker. More like a young professor in a long coat, someone you might see in the Village in New York early in spring, and instead of a high-tech aluminum walking stick, he carried a knobby wooden stick he leaned on like a cane. I remember how quickly I raced to get out my camera. It was one of those passing moments that seemed to be perfectly composed. Lost in thought, he had one foot propped up on a rock and was looking down at a valley shrouded in mist. In places, little blocky rocks poked up through the gray shroud. In the distance there were mountains, some high and rounded, and some spiky and vertical.

In fact, the scene was perfectly composed, though I think I was the last one to see why. Coming home to Philadelphia after my trip, a friend said,

"Oh my God, it's Caspar Frederick's Wanderer Above the Sea of Fog. *Don't you know that painting? The one with the aristocrat in the top coat, looking down from the top of a mountain. You even give him the same walking stick!"*

It turned out that the painting was so famous I didn't have to know it; that in some way it was part of me even though I had never seen it, or perhaps, never remembered having seen it.

Her narrative is plain and clear, but its plainness and clarity derive from a simple embedded structure of seeing, feeling, and thinking. She sees a scene. She describes her feelings in seeing it, and something of her surprise in being told that the scene resembles another scene. And she began the process of thinking about it. This passage became the opening of her admissions essay.

I was able to help her further along this process by giving her a few more readings. I chose Freud's 1911 essay on creativity, an early piece by Carl Jung about the imagery of the collective unconscious, and a chapter from John Berger's *Ways of Seeing* (1972). We spent about six more weeks reading these, after which she was able to move from good seeing rooted in a self-awareness of feeling to the beginnings of clear, grounded thought:

After reading Freud's essay, I am starting to think that there is an artistic unconscious. I'm not sure it's collective the way Carl Jung said it was (I think it has to be individually acquired), and I'm not sure where it comes from, but I know from my own experience that I am an archive of images I am barely aware of. I am a carrier of icons. There seems to be a kind of inner order in images, and I am now trying to find out what it is. A very important book for me has been Rudolf Arnheim's Art and Visual Perception. *Arnheim writes,*

It no longer seemed possible to think of vision as proceeding from the particular to the general. On the contrary, it became evident that overall structural features are the primary data of perception.

This only sounds abstract. I have felt this. I saw it in that picture I took at Glacier. Understanding how and why I took that picture has, for the first time in my life, energized me with an idea. The idea of the structure of the image, of how it holds together and how it works in our minds, one at a time, is what makes me want to go to college. No, not want to, need to: I now feel I need to study all the fields that make Arnheim's book as good as it is: psychology, cognitive science, philosophy, art history, and literature. I have no idea where these will take me. Farther into myself, yes, but also deeper into one of the grounding elements of what it means to be human.

The subjects she lists here bring up the question of range. High schools introduce only a narrow range of disciplines. A student interested in a subject rarely taught in high school can often pass unrecognized. The sad fact is that each of the major fields she mentions are usually absent in high school: psychology, anthropology, philosophy, art history, architecture, sociology, the various areas of ethnic studies, and all but a few languages. High schools often take a synoptic approach to knowledge, laying out a large map at a low level of resolution. But many find that nothing in this flat map interests them, partly because knowledge mapped at this scale always distorts it to some extent like a single line on a map representing a stream or a road or a point representing a city. Much of my work amounts to getting students to look at small areas of knowledge in greater and greater detail. These areas may or may not take hold, but they find it exhilarating to feel an interest in an academic subject whose presentation is not simplified in scale or extent.

It is often hard for students to talk about an interest that leads into fields of which they may be completely unaware. But a real direction often begins with a vague formulation of it. "I kind of like" only sounds tentative. It shows a student starting to sense more than she could possibly say about her own direction, beginning to discover unknown elements of herself. Part of my role is to give a more accurate picture of the order of things as seen from the university. Part is to help students find the orderliness of observations and directions that exists in their own experience, giving them fresh subjects that correspond to their own incipient directions. Simply seeing their own developing interests reflected somewhere at the university makes for a good beginning.

The photographer went on to study art history. Our work did not take us that far. I helped her see only that she liked thinking about the history and structure of images and to take her experiencing of that idea all the way to the limit. No larger direction came out of it. The application she submitted was open-ended, saying she might conceivably study art, architecture, film, media, or design.

But in our work, she found herself involved in a new dimension of herself. Experiencing ideas as arising from the quick of her own observation, then having to question that evidence, seeing how it had been shaped and distorted by tradition, made her stand apart from herself, seeing herself as an active rather than a passive observer. It made her very aware that she could not see all that her senses reported. What did she see that day at Glacier? She saw the things that fit the mental picture she carried around of them, and she placed those things in the photograph she took. In our work together, she found a pattern, an underlying order, in her perception. Her essay was able to begin tracing that pattern, and for her college application, that beginning was good enough.

~~~~~~~~~~

My second case is about a figure skater who came to me saying that he had given up skating. He said his interests had taken an academic turn. He then started talking about those interests. His account of them drifted from a novel he read to a biography, lightly perused, of Olympic runner Jesse Owens. After a while, I began to see how thin those interests were and that really, since giving up skating, he had mostly been drifting from topic to topic, reading a little here, a little there, but always losing interest.

I began to ask why he was drifting in the first place. It all came back to leaving the rink. His life used to be fully taken up with figure skating. Then he dropped it. Why?

I asked him to write an account of it. Initially, he wrote:

The dance was an Argentine tango. The dance begins with partners in open hold for steps one to ten. I started out with the usual chassé and progressive sequence to bring my partner to a bold LFO edge by step seven. Then, on eight, both of us skated a right forward outside cross, holding it for one beat. The tempo was set at 96 beats per minute, and my partner and I had one minute and ten seconds to skate two sequences.

This has the smooth flow of expert commentary, but without that expertise, the scene cannot easily be visualized. In fact, he derived it from the manner of spoken commentary on television, where the ongoing image of the skater makes it possible for the commentator to sound "expert" without actually explaining anything. This is why television commentators usually come in pairs, one full of jargon, and one not. When I asked him to explain just what an LFO edge and a right forward outside cross were, he used other unfamiliar terms, talking about kilians, cross rolls, and edge-changes. Listening, I came to see that his feeling for the sport was physical and not verbal. The moves on the ice were for him a matter of muscle memory. The terms were precise but incidental to his actual experience of motion on the ice. So, I decided to show him a lovely book I knew about, *The Skater's Manual*, written in 1867. It abounds in clear descriptions of moves on the ice:

The Dutch Traveling Roll is the plan by which Hollanders travel on the ice. Starting from the right foot, leaning to the outside, keep the knee straight, and, with the left foot behind the right, describe a half circle, or rather a part of one. When this is completed, bring the right into a similar position, and, with the toe close to the ice, commence a similar strike, and then these successive strokes will describe a small segment of a very large circle.

Here, the description achieves a plain visual resolution. A reader can easily picture a scene like one from a painting by Breughel. It succeeds because it is a visual image set into motion, phrase by phrase. After reading it, he was able to write the sentence:

My upper body leaned forward at a slight angle to lead the female in a classic slinging motion.

Here, no technical terms are used. None are needed. The image of the sling is enough for the reader to begin to see the routine, and describing it as "classic" shows that the move is well-known among skaters. This is certainly good seeing, but still it lacks emotional presence. His next efforts at writing were about recovering feeling. This was hard for him. We had to talk about it for several sessions before he said, very quietly, "I didn't tell you what happened, did I? That day."

"What day?" I asked.

"The day outside the North Stars stadium. After the exhibition."

He paused.

"I stopped skating after that."

Then he told me. It turned out he had been harassed by a gang of teenage boys, North Stars fans, leaving the area after a skating exhibition. He did not talk easily about what had happened. I asked him to write about it. He wrote several accounts. His voice was powerful and direct:

The boys were ugly. They were going to be fat someday and they knew it. I don't think they were drunk but they were somehow wanting to act drunk, like being loud and jaunty was a goal for them. And they were mean. My God, they were mean.

*"You're a girl, you know that. Those aren't black skates. They oughta be white with pink frills. The whole thing is so—*female!*"*

This was still as yet too raw to be useful for a college essay. It turned out the reason he wrote about an Argentine tango is that it had been his last dance. He never skated again after that day. In our work, he had initially substituted the procedure of the dance for his experience of it, but in his mind, the two were bound together deeply. He then told me why he had not finished the biography of Jesse Owens. "It was just too painful—those Nazis jeering at him at the 1936 Olympics." Encouraging him to look again at the biography—for Owens had transcended the hatred directed at him—I worked with him to develop an account of the incident true in both seeing and feeling. Working with the two books, he was, after a few weeks, able to write a narrative blending the two strains into one:

The dance was a tango. A tango on ice is hard enough for two skaters, but to do it with only one took a lot of thought. I first wanted to take on both parts at once, but my coach, Dix Benson, mindful of the mistakes that had cost him the gold at Nagano, had me set up a gender-shifting routine in which I would take first the male part, then the female, then return again to the male. I brought together the whole routine for the first time at the 2008 national in Minneapolis. I began with the male part. My upper body leaned forward at a slight angle to lead the female in a classic slinging motion. I had to show her contortion while myself remaining fairly rigid. Dix said if I did it right the audience would feel like I was controlling the girl like a puppet. Then I began my move into the female part, raising and twisting my right leg to look like a woman wrapping her leg around a man. Then I snapped back into the upright male posture, my left arm facing the judge, and glided slowly toward the bright yellow exit.

I was leaning over the rail, catching my breath, my sleeves drenched and my hands purple. I wasn't feeling very focused, but when I looked up a boy was looking at me from the other side of the rail. He was twelve, thirteen maybe. When he saw me noticing his stare he turned away and said to his friends,

"Let's get out of here. This whole thing is so—female."

This is good narrative, integrating the seeing and feeling that had been separate in the early drafts, but it as yet lacks a developed thought. A tilt of thought can be sensed under the surface of the story, which clearly implicates definitions of gender. So, I introduced him to Simone de Beauvoir's *The Second Sex* (1948). There she writes:

In the mouth of a man the epithet female has the sound of an insult, yet he is not ashamed of his animal nature; on the contrary, he is proud if someone says of him: "He is a male!" The term "female" is derogatory not because it emphasizes woman's animality, but because it imprisons her in her sex.

And so, taking this in, he was able to add, some weeks later:

I thought about this for a long time. I kept thinking about a book I'd read recently, The Second Sex *by Simone de Beauvoir. One of the first things she said was, "In the mouth of a male the epithet female has the sound of an insult." And here it was in full blown form. I had trained for eight years to get as far as the Minneapolis national, and here, the compass of everything I'd done had been compressed into a single epithet. Beauvoir goes on to say that you're not born into a gender. You're created into one. The body is not a thing, she observes, but a situation, and it was such a situation that I was confronted with on the ice in Minneapolis. What I was seeing was not the final product of gender but the making of gender through an imagined consensus among three boys. I certainly felt the force of the insult, but now I came to realize I was also witnessing a little theater of their own individual projections in which they were in the process of imagining their gender for themselves. I was actually only a minor part of it, a helpless catalyst in a process that can be enacted in a hundred different ways and yet still possess its regularities. It began now to occur to me: what are those regularities, and how could they be reconstructed?*

I soon found that this took me beyond the bounds of de Beauvoir's book, and even to the edges of feminism.

Here at last, seeing, feeling, and thinking come together. Skating is an action seen, a practice felt, and a sport with a sociology to be thought about. Note how carefully he avoids affiliating himself with Beauvoir's feminism. He is not positioning himself as a feminist, but using elements of feminist thought in an analytical context. He uses a thinker without being used by her, without allowing the force and depth of her thought to completely condition his own. The tone throughout the essay remains emotional, but this emotion is held in check by good seeing and restrained thinking. This was for my student a real achievement. In speaking about leaving skating, his voice broke, his hands trembled, and his eyes filmed with tears. The essay similarly has an emotional valence throughout. When he reaches Beauvoir, it is clear to the reader that her ideas are for him no mere set of abstractions. He told me he was often teased at school for carrying around such a thick book. He said he responded by reading them passages from the book, choosing them so effectively that other students in the school began to be seen carrying around *The Second Sex*.

"The library had to order extra copies," he told me with quiet pride.

He never went back into skating, but he began seriously to pursue gender studies, and later, majored in anthropology.

~~~~~~~~~~~~

My third case is an object lesson of thought in isolation. My student wanted to be a marine biologist. She was a diver who had spent part of a summer at Moss Landing Marine Labs in Monterey, California. Coming to me, she was beginning to read around in the scientific literature of her field. She had a draft of her essay, which opened:

Research has shown that the nitrogen-ammonia balance in certain environments can change the key role of invertebrates in mediating dominance of a foundation species. Associated taxa such as Cladophora columbiana *can often effect host performance.*

And so on. Here, our writer is getting ahead of herself. She is trying to mimic the language of a scientific article without offering any genuine insight based on real research of her own. The felt underlay of her own experience is missing, as is any sense of observation. This element of voice need not be entirely discarded. She is beginning to hear what a scientist should sound like and is imitating that sound. Starting over again, I gave her a passage from chapter 16 of Charles Darwin's *The Voyage of the Beagle* (1839):

I spent some days in examining the step-formed terraces of shingle, first noticed by Captain B. Hall, and believed by Mr. Lyell to have been formed by the sea during the gradual rising of the land. This certainly is the true explanation, for I found numerous shells of existing species on these terraces.

Here, the writer has a clear, moderate voice. He sees some terraces, modestly saying it had been pointed out to him by Captain Hall, and talks about Lyell's work on sedimentary environments. Only then does he return to the scene, continuing to vest it with the immediacy of his own close observation:

Five narrow, gently sloping, fringe-like terraces rise one behind the other, and where best developed are formed of shingle: they front the bay, and sweep up both sides of the valley. At Guasco, north of Coquimbo, the phenomenon is displayed on a much grander scale, so as to strike with surprise even some of the inhabitants. The terraces are there much broader, and may be called plains, in some parts there are six of them, but generally only five; they run up the valley for thirty-seven miles from the coast. These step-formed terraces or fringes closely resemble those in the valley of S. Cruz, and, except in being on a smaller scale, those great ones along the whole coast-line of Patagonia. They have undoubtedly been formed by the denuding power of the sea, during long periods of rest in the gradual elevation of the continent.

I then asked her what the name of the research vessel was at Moss Landing. She said, "The John H. Martin." So, I asked her, using Darwin as a point of reference, to try and write *The Voyage of the John H. Martin.* This is what she came up with:

The John H. Martin was docked at the end of the jetty in Moss Landing, California. The boat was not much larger than a small tugboat, with a slight upsweep of the hull at its prow. It had a small cabin for the captain and the professor, but otherwise the boat was all deck. Before setting off for the Elkhorn Slough, we had to stow all the new equipment that would soon be deployed for research. One case reminded me of ones that held microscopes at school, an odd looking white tube encased in metal scaffolding.

This passage is scientific observation applied to the act of description. Though vivid, it lacks situation and deep emotional purpose. The writer has jumped from thinking to seeing, bypassing feeling entirely, and eliminating thinking in the process. Note how only the boat is described. There are no people here, just a boat, and no sense of any ground of human emotion. Nor is there any real sense of geographical setting. The passage is now physically vivid, but it still lacks a force of emotion or a sense of intellectual focus. With this student, it took me many weeks to get her to begin to think about what she was feeling while she was doing something. It was a difficult step for her. Since she was a little girl, she had always known what she wanted to do—to become a marine biologist—and her life so far had been focused on doing it. She writes with a certain blunt determination, but her sense of why she was deciding to do it was absent until the very last drafts, where she was able to write:

Cold water rushed into my wetsuit. Leaning over the side of the boat, the attendant handed me the clipboard with the pencil and pointed me toward the survey site. The water was warm and had low visibility. Going down, patches of cold water currents mixed with warmer water currents. Two meters underwater, hard corals thrived.

I swam toward the beginning point of the transect, hovering just above the corals.

Here are good seeing and feeling; what remained was adding good thinking. The thinking had to be not an add-on but a necessary growth from what was seen and felt. She at first wrote a number of passages that quoted technical findings from a 2007 article by Matthew Bracken and several other scientists called "Whole-Community Mutualism." These went to the nitrogen-ammonia balance found in certain corals. But the description was flat and dry. I told her she needed to approach the corals gradually, setting the scene so the reader could see what she saw. It took much effort for her to write:

There were vast stretches of sandy bottoms below the boat. I could just make out patches of corals. I swam toward the beginning point of the transect, hovering just above the corals. The transect was to be defined by a long length of yellow tape, marked at intervals of ten meters. Below me, I saw an abundance of invertebrates living on the surfaces and crannies of healthy corals. I kept a careful eye out for any sign of whitening in the corals. Anything but white is healthy, I remembered telling myself, remembering a classic article by Matthew Bracken on the mutualism between Cladophora, *a species of seaweed, and associated invertebrates. So, when I began to see long stretches of bleached white corals, I knew that something was very wrong.*

She then went on to say why, quoting a bit more from the article. She also tries to add to Bracken's research by looking for other signs of environmental damage. She calls these "index signs," and though she comes to no clear conclusion, she comes across as a motivated and determined young researcher. This is important in an application for marine biology, which often sees applications from students who have taken up diving as hobby and like being around the sea. Reading her application, one almost forgets she is working underwater, because she is so focused on the work at hand. She does not confuse the means of scientific research with its ends.

My work with her involved little clarification of her aims. But it took her some time to see that she was not writing for a scientific audience, though someday she might. Here, my concern was not in writing toward the work, to elicit it, but in writing about it, shifting her voice to address a larger audience. I did not need to recommend any reading to her other than the Darwin; she quoted fluently from articles she knew very well. What she needed was to use the integrative capacity of good prose to show herself fully operating in the three dimensions of seeing, feeling, and thinking. Her scientific voice, based as it was on an imitation of the sound of scientific articles and not on any original research of her own, was derivative. Her own voice was absent. Only after a layering of drafts was she able to show, at last, a delicate and sensitive awareness of the natural world that had not been screened through the conceptual filter of formal scientific language. It was precisely this sense of discovery that was lacking in her early drafts. It made her application come alive because it accesses the full potential of what she saw and felt, as well as what she thought.

~~~~~~~~~~~

Admissions is rarely studied in individual cases. Some startling examples make the newspapers, but these rarely look at the cases with a highly resolved degree of focus. To the extent that admissions comes under scrutiny at all, the individual tends to be seen as part of the lump sums of groups or as exceptions that, by implication, prove the rule, whatever that may be said to be.

Certainly, many applications share things in common. The experiences in each of these three cases are not far outside of the common run of experience. Taking pictures on a trip, skating in a competition, going on a dive. In each case, the writers began their narratives with shared experience, so much so, that it was hard to tell their particular experiences apart from anyone else's. The narratives had a blended duality that evened out the irregularities of personal experience. In each of the early drafts, a personal knowing hardly exists. It lacks the fullness of particularity. In each case, it took me some time to convince them that their actual experience could not be fully accounted for in their first attempts to narrate it.

These narratives are often halting at first. Signs of a new integration can easily pass unnoticed in a mass of mediocre writing. They are rarely recognized as such. I find that my most basic form of intervention comes simply in telling them when they have written well and then proceeding to prove it to them, point by point. For very few students can see when they have come to something new. Even at Harvard, I often felt my role as a tutor was often simply to say, "There's only one great sentence in this paper. Keep it, throw the rest away, and start *right here.*" Right here: a good sentence has a degree of rightness and hereness that is premonitory. Each of my three students had a breakthrough sentence, a single striking statement of a new way of being in writing in which seeing, feeling, and thinking attained a unity. In these three cases the sentences were:

It turned out that the painting was so famous I didn't have to know it; that in some way it was part of me even though I had never seen it, or perhaps, never remembered having seen it.

I had trained for eight years to get as far as the Minneapolis national, and here, the compass of everything I'd done had been compressed into a single epithet.

Cold water rushed into my wetsuit.

A look above at what they were able to do with them shows just how much of their new direction was embedded in a single statement. The statement was anything but an epiphany to them; in fact, that word can be very misleading in this context, because not one of the three experienced their leap in development as an epiphany. For most of them, it was just another sentence they wrote. I found I had to show them how good they were and how they led the way. I began showing them sentences by good writers that do similar things, to show them what good company they were in. Then I often asked them to google the best phrases in their sentence, putting quotation marks around them to make the search highly specific. When the answer came up, "No result; no match found," I could demonstrate to them that, at last, here was the grain of their own voice. It might have been only a beginning, but it was a solid beginning, and a real one, that was all their own.

Every student I have ever worked with would make a good case study. I have only chosen three here, mostly because, like the essays about the mine and the orange, they represent clear general patterns or tendencies. Most of my students start with a good ground in seeing, feeling, or thinking, and their progress is additive, though in what way I can never predict.

~~~~~~~~~~

Seeing, feeling, thinking. Again and again, we have seen that, in good writing, there is a strong tendency toward exactness in differentiation of seeing, feeling, and thinking. After a few months of work with me, my students share a common goal: using writing to capture something they have not seen (or seen in passing) or felt (without understanding the feeling) about their own experience. Writing becomes a means by which they can listen to themselves, checking what they used to say about themselves against the direct referent of their own experience recorded in good prose. I often hear something like, "It's funny. I used to say this about myself, but now that I look at it again, I'm not like this at all." In each case, good writing led the writer to a more evolved, more accurate self-image. They start to see things differently by probing experiences that prove to be sharply at variance with prior ideas of self. They begin the process by thinking (and often telling me outright) that they don't see the point of plumbing one narrow segment of experience. Gradually they come to appreciate that a well-understood moment of experience becomes a referent against which any idea about it can be tested. Becoming closer to one experience helps them along their way to becoming closer to the unfolding of all experiences. The acts of seeing, feeling, and thinking become much more highly differentiated and nuanced. They feel, at last, ready to begin education as a course of action they have chosen constructively rather than defensively, ready to make adjustments to new as well as old conditions, making going to college a natural forward motion.

8

The Narrative-Based Application

THE BASIC idea of this book is that writing shows the writer the way into college. I want now to carry that idea outside the essay and show how, once a transformation can be sensed in the prose itself, the essay can begin to lead in a meaningful way to new directions outside it.

The essay shifts the locus of choices and decisions to the writer. The writer increasingly comes to feel that what he or she does in the world should be actively chosen rather than passively received. Many students often come to me complaining that few of the activities they take part in at school have any deep meaning for them. They are very aware that their schools offer a fixed number of these, clubs, sports, bands, and theatricals, and they often feel forced to make the best choice they can among them. There is nothing wrong with these activities. It is just that they do not come *from* the student, and they rarely lead to the discovery of unknown tendencies and directions. The word is itself telling: "Activity" means something designed to keep you active. This is only a small step above being busy for its own sake, and it is equally telling that the word is often used in the plural, as though one thing pursued deeply in and for itself is never enough.

As the essay becomes the leading edge of a student's development, it should drive how the student uses his or her time outside school. By this, I mean that the essay, once well underway, should begin to provide a coordinating frame for what a student does after school, on weekends, and during summers. Our two essays are again exemplary. The student at the mine decides to take a trip with their father back to the mine. The student peeling the orange goes ahead and takes a course in field geology at the University of Georgia. These external directions add *doing* to seeing and feeling and thinking. They bring the sense of being active, rather than passive, back into the idea of activities. The essay is the proving ground. As it develops, it creates extensions out of itself and leads to action. The scope of that action is often very limited. It can be a single trip or a line of research into a single, limited subject. What matters is that the action is congruent with the essay's matching of observation, feeling, and thought.

This has to be true at all levels of the application. Reading it, one must have the sense that the writer is one unified person all the way along. I have already said how, when writing works well, any experience observed carries both feeling and thought with it. When the application is similarly congruent, there is a sense of the presence of the writer's seeing, feeling, and thinking felt strongly everywhere as the reader reads. The best writers always have this in their books, which have long been admired for their strongly integrated voices.

What I have found is that it is possible to carry over this integration of voice into the whole of an application so that each of its parts have a wholeness in and of themselves. I do not see them as interlocking pieces of a puzzle. The pieces of a puzzle, taken by themselves, speak very little, and they always await being assembled before they can deliver their message. Rather, I see each piece as a completely genuine marker of a whole whose wholeness is seen and confirmed again and again each time another part of the application is read.

This is why the short parts of the application are just as important as the long parts. All should form part of the application's master narrative. Recall that a good master narrative of an application has a clear voice, a good central story, and an integration of related stories. I have already covered voice and story at length. They form the foundation of the narrative-based application.

But the central defining feature of the narrative-based application is a purposeful integration of voice and story *across* the various documents of the application. This includes all the answers to every question, no matter how small or cursory. The voice and the stories remain both separate and inseparably woven together. The narrative-based application extends the application's master narrative into all the other parts of the application, often in unexpected ways. This includes not just the essays, long and short, but also many after-school activities, travel, summers, work, classes, independent study, and letters of recommendation.

Any activity can provide a starting point from which clear, individual choices may emerge. Visiting a mine on a class trip may provoke a long train of thought. Playing an instrument may lead to an interest in music theory and history. Taking a role in a play may lead to an interest in drama or foreign languages. But at some point, the student must show some sign of becoming self-directed. Students need to come to see themselves differently through these activities, seeing new directions that are particular to the individual. A student who took up the cello may decide to switch to the cello's predecessor, the viola da gamba. A student may start with one language and change to another because it is more resonant with them in some way. What matters here is a student becoming more open to individual experience, both internally and externally.

Not all activities can or should be included in a master narrative. Only those which form the basis of the student's direction are really relevant here. Packing a résumé has the effect of cluttering it and making it hard to see how anything can emerge from such a mass of unrelated actions. Nearing college, a few students have already begun this winnowing process, but many have not. I find that in many cases I have to help a student sort through masses of affiliations to find which ones are really binding. Usually when an activity begins to take hold within a student, he or she begins to develop a highly independent path within it. By "independent," I mean a realistic independence that is age appropriate. Within any given activity, the more independent the direction, the better, but only within limits. Students should adopt realistic goals for themselves, showing that they are capable of moving stepwise toward a foreseeable end. Small, careful steps are best, showing an increasing matching of experience with awareness, of doing with being. A class one level above what is offered in high school. A shift from classical music to jazz. A movement from a general concern with "social justice" to a particular involvement in a specific political issue.

Our student at the mine took a school-sponsored trip to West Virginia. But, in looking at the first draft, the writer realized it was important to see the mine again. Here is where a writer's determination matters. Realizing that not everything has been seen and suspecting, too, that much may have been seen wrongly, the writer goes back to the mine a second time. The writer describes it in a short answer to a typical supplemental question about travel experiences:

I went back to the mine a second time by myself. Or almost. My father drove me. He said he did not want me driving through mountain roads alone. He made sure that I called ahead of time so that a representative from a mine could meet us there. I told him I knew just the man, because in a way, I felt I knew him.

It turned out his name was Ogden Fillbrook. I thought right away of the nearby Monongahela River filled with muddy slurry from the mine. It felt strangely fictional, as though Charles Dickens had made up his name for one of his novels.

But he was real enough. He met us at the gate and gave us passes and shiny yellow helmets with VISITOR stenciled in interrupted letters on the back rim. He asked us if we were hungry. I was but said no.

"There's Cokes and Mars bars here," he said apologetically. "Not much else."

I said I didn't want any but he seemed glad that my father did. I saw how he let his hand rest on my father's wrist for a moment longer than it had to. I thought: He wants to feel some connection to us. He wants to get to know us a little. He's not a bad guy.

I have already said how important the phrase "I looked again" is. Here, looking again means taking a second trip to the mine. In this, the writer is active and self-directed. Just the fact of being alone, or nearly alone, means being more open to what is being seen. It can, of course, be frightening. Looking again means being aware that one has not seen all there is to see the first time. Looking again means wondering what is actually going on. And looking again means looking tentatively at something as though for the very first time. An essay does not necessarily need to project a complete understanding of something. It can show the writer trying to understanding something by leaving a private perceptual world and entering, or at least trying to enter, into those of others. It involves being sensitive to changes that happen moment by moment, without making judgments.

This second seeing also reverberates in other ways with our writer. Coming home, the writer starts to act with even greater independence. In an answer to another supplemental question, again a fairly typical question about activities, the writer takes the opportunity to return to the master narrative and its larger implications for life:

Going to the mine a second time, I felt that the whole trip left something unsaid. It wasn't that I asked the wrong questions. I didn't even know what the right questions were. So during student elections two months later, I set up a little table in the Forum under the heading, Questioning Mining. *I also interviewed a lot of people who went there with me the first time and tried to ask them what they saw. And I set up a little exhibit of books from the library on mining and its history in the United States.*

Strange thing was, I became a write-in candidate for student president. I don't know who came up with the idea. I didn't win, of course, but I came in a strong second, so they put me on student council, where I organized a third trip to the mine, this one led by the miners I'd met the second time. Later the school paper ran a special issue about it.

This passage takes on meaning partly by reverberation. Because this is part of the master narrative, the writer does not need to sound out every note of the main story here. The passage is able to be short yet resonant. These smaller stories are like partial harmonics in music, where any voicing of a stringed instrument consists of a number of other pitches, reverberations of the strings at intervals, thirds and fifths and sixths, which, superimposed on the main tone, add depth, dimension, and color—in a word, *voice*—to the sound of the instrument. The main tone still carries the main impact of the sound, just as the longer essay still carries the main burden of the seeing, feeling, and thinking. Precisely because we have read it and have a sense of its range, we become able to experience other vibrations in that narrative—so that this little piece strikes us as a resonant part of a whole, larger narrative. The resonance may even be a little dissonant sometimes, as in music. But overall, it strikes us as beautifully *congruent*.

Here is our student with the orange, answering a supplemental question by telling a story about a hobby developed as a child:

As a child, I never went swimming at the beach in Ocean City. I used to build sand castles then watch them erode. A few years later I came on the idea of hitting the ground with a shovel to see if I could make them fall over by making the beach tremble. I kept wondering how hard I'd have to pound the ground to get the walls to crack. I even took notes.

So for my twelfth birthday, my parents gave me a toy seismograph. It was called a Hubbard Scientific Seismograph—basically a roll of paper hooked up to a pen on a wire. When you pounded the ground the wire jiggled and made lines on the paper. It wasn't easy to pull out the paper at a constant rate, but working at it, I soon had a jagged little record of things that jiggled.

I used it on everything. Passing trucks rattling the house. The washing machine spinning out of control. The back seat of the car over a gravel road. The paper was not graph paper but I made up numbers that looked sort of right to me.

I became known in the neighborhood as "the kid with the seismograph." I was proud of the name. I still am.

It may happen that a student's real direction first appears as play rather than work. A full mental world can often be hidden in a hobby. Model railroads are full of engineering. Fashion is full of art history. Origami is deeply geometrical. The importance of these pastimes can often be invisible to a student because they often feel they should not be doing them, or that in doing them, they are somehow taking something away from their academic work. Yet these can often be little secret gardens, private imaginative worlds that can be beneficially plumbed for real directions in a college application.

~~~~~~~~~~~

What should a student do with an activity that cannot fit into the master narrative they have devised? Almost anything can be wound into a narrative by a strong narrative voice; think of any novel and the range of experience it may include. One class of activity, however, often resists inclusion in a college application and can seem incongruent with the whole. This is the special case of sports.

Many of my students have loved a sport since childhood. Few will become professional athletes, but many still enjoy mastering a complex physical activity. Many stay with it even though the sport slowly takes over their lives, using up most of their spare time, dampening their grades, and making study difficult because they are so tired after practice. Few of these students understand that very few of the best colleges and universities have a deep standing culture of sport. Students on athletic scholarships to Ivy League schools often arrive to find their position in the campus culture to be marginal. Celebrated in high school, they find themselves invisible in college. They often turn to their team for a sense of identity rather than to the college at large. The culture of sport is almost never an intellectual culture, and many student athletes find themselves at the margins of the academic community.

A certain corruption pervades the admission of athletes, but only the best ones. The students I see are mostly good athletes but not great ones. They often find that continuing with a sport after their sophomore year offers diminishing returns. A summer spent at a sports camp is a summer *not* spent taking a class, initiating a research project, or learning a new language. From year to year, my student athletes find they fall further and further behind their peers in amassing specifically academic achievements. Many of them will often try to build a master narrative out of their interest in a sport, saying they want to go into sports medicine or journalism. But most of the best colleges are not nearly so specialized at the undergraduate level, and in any case, this rationale is so overused, and so commonly strained, that it is unconvincing. Stories that try to draw lessons from sports applicable to the classroom can often sound like a locker-room pep talk rather than a college application. Here, a student athlete is confronted with a very mature choice. They have one dominant interest, purely nonacademic, that will not advance their others. There is no easy out. At a certain point, most will need to make more time to study. I can never tell a student when to make the decision to leave off playing a sport. I simply present them with the likely consequences of a decision they must make on their own.

~~~~~~~~~~

The extension of the master narrative into the whole application is anything but rhetorical or artificial. The master narrative is a *saying*. The narrative of the narrative-based application extends the *saying* into a *doing*. A story, however well told, can seem distant and set somewhere in the past. The narrative takes on a very active tilt by showing the student taking a hard-won self-understanding into the realm of the larger world. This world can be a larger political or cultural world, but it begins to draw lines of affiliation between small personal insights and the larger forces of life. It takes the way of being represented in the essays and places it as a way of being in the world. It works toward placing the writer in a position in the world.

A very particular kind of position. D. W. Winnicott speaks of the three lives of a person. A life in the world, a life of cultural experience, and a life of the personal. They are three nested circles. The outer circle, the largest, includes city, state, and country. The middle circle takes in cultural and ethnic identity. The smallest inner circle is the inner life of the individual.

College applications mostly feature a life in the world and, recently, have added a life of cultural experience. But the life of the personal has been relegated to the "personal" essay, which is sometimes impersonal in all but name because it often amounts to a mere recapitulation of a student's life in the world, adding to it, at times, a light smattering of cultural experience. The life of the personal then has to be read between the lines of the life in the world and a cultural life. A life in a world includes civic and political life. A cultural life includes family, race, and religion. But the final picture given by these is always a little blurred, because, as Winnicott says, not that much is required to inhabit the identity of a group. I have often had the experience of picking through the draft of a personal essay, trying hard to find anything *personal* in it. The means of expression are often absent. A life in the world delivers up a kind of résumé. A life of cultural experience often easily turns into a received narrative that may or may not reveal the inner life of the writer. In such cases, the actual feelings of students come out as small, marginal moments in which the writer actually manages to *see* something instead of perceiving it through preconditioned categories.

I have tried to show at length how I work with these moments to draw out a vivid life of the personal in which the student takes the evidence of his or her own life as it is rather than adjusting it to fit a preexisting pattern. A life in the world and a life in a culture can only speak partially to a life of the personal. It takes a long time to instill in a young writer a genuine openness to experience, where self-knowledge, rather than self-placement in existing cultural categories, becomes central. Just think of the meaning embedded in that common term, college *placement*. It means the action of placing someone instead of them placing themselves. It also has a rigid feeling like putting a brick in a wall, a feeling of putting someone in a particular place for good. There is little sense of elasticity of choice behind the word *placement*. One story I have heard over and over again from my students is about going to see a college counselor, who usually has a little foreshortened list of choices made out. It is rarely binding, but it is always directive, and few students like the feeling of having their most fundamental choices made for them in advance. They often come to me saying, "Is this all?"

It is not.

Admissions today tends to devolve on groups, with new, underrepresented groups replacing old, overrepresented ones. Many students, in choosing something to write about, will take a collective experience first. Our writer at the mine did this. But we have seen that it becomes very hard to discover the underlying reality of any given application when the forms of external representation dictated by a life in the world, plus a cultural life, effectively obscure the life of the personal. The sad fact is that collective experience can make individual experience hard to find. I have seen for myself that writing about belonging to any group, as part of almost any activity, often dampens the sharpness of individual perception. The causality here works in a circle, with students simplifying themselves as members of groups, and admissions committees, in turn, relying on means that simplify the students by their membership in those groups.

In this chapter, I have made the case for a way around this circle. The narrative-based application makes students three-dimensional by developing them as writers *across* the application. By now it should be clear that I see writing as the joint form for *individual* seeing, feeling, and thinking. David Hume, from whom I have derived much of my own thinking, writes that "it is impossible for us to *think* of any thing, which we have not antecedently *felt*, either by our external or internal senses." The power of the narrative-based application resides in pinpointing the origin of thinking in seeing and feeling, in material and psychological fact. It makes thought concrete in a way that any high school junior or senior can understand. Its results may be approximate at best, but it is at least clear as to the origin of those approximations. This is the striking thread we are able to draw between the fine examples of essays by literary writers and between the student essays whose development I have been tracing in this book. As narrative, one can distrust the conclusions a writer reaches without necessarily distrusting *how* the writer reached them. The integrity of a voice can easily survive the recognition that it is not omniscient and that sometimes, immersed in the rush of events, the writer may get some things wrong. What matters is not what is right or wrong but the integrity of the effort itself, the *trying*, which is at the heart of Montaigne's use of *essayer*, the French verb for "to try," in his classic *Essays*.

A legitimate hesitation here goes to the nature of narrative itself. Narrative is not fact. Narrative tilts to the subjective and blends easily into story. Many personal essays are already so personal or so fictional that it is hard to find anything to hold onto when reading them. The makers of the Scholastic Aptitude Test come right out and admit they do not have the time to check the facts for any of the essays in the writing section. Too much already passes unexamined. Why ask for more?

The answer lies in *more*. The more writing is asked for in an application, the more its readers have some basis for comparison. A short essay can get away with stretching the truth because it does not have space to stretch it too far. But a long essay stretching the truth snaps it at some point. As a sustained piece of work, the application cannot be easily gamed. Nor can it be written quickly. Think of the difference between one page of writing and ten. A long essay has to conform to certain canons of internal coherence. A passing citation may be passed over, but an extended example is a sustained piece of evidence. A short essay standing alone can be a short-term bluff. But a series of related essays encourages greater order, greater coordination, and greater integration.

Another objection lies in the difficulty of the project. A considerable number of students are likely to fall far short of a robust master narrative. The sad fact is that many students are not, and will never be, good writers. They may tell stories about themselves which, though couched in clichés, have considerable meaning for them. This meaning springs from their own individual experience, which for them is only partially and imperfectly communicable in language. What do we do with a student whose experience is lived rather than understood, whose awareness is partial, and whose reflex to life is conditioned by the force of habit rather than observation?

This is a problem that the narrative-based application cannot solve but can address. Many students who block off from their narrative awareness of large areas of experience may yet have an area in which they are capable of a more accurate picture of life. Careful readers may be able to detect signs of an incipient awareness of a larger range of perception. The best that can be said about the method of the narrative-based application is that it is precisely a *method* and not an outcome. That is, it produces data of a wholly different order than grades or scores, which have been filtered through so many different lenses of interpretation that a high degree of distortion is inevitable. No single test measures scholastic aptitude, no more than any single course does. Because a high degree of competence with language is central to success at the university, the clearest possible measure of it will carry the most predictive value. A narrative-based application will not relieve committees of making hard decisions and difficult guesses. It will only help them make the decisions more fine-grained, and the guesses more informed.

It also changes the experience of the students themselves. Completing a whole application, they feel completely whole. The coherence and organization they have brought to it are not a superimposition but their own. For many, it is the first time they have learned how to do something without molding themselves into a pattern provided by a teacher. The process often unfolds with great intensity as they work at being close to themselves, to their own observation and feeling, as they write. They find themselves saying things they really want to say, speaking from deep within themselves; and, just as importantly, they find themselves saying things they did not know they had it in them to say. Learning how to write beyond their conscious intent, they start to see how their deepest feelings often lead to their best ideas. One thing I often hear is, "I feel I've never really written anything until now. I feel like I'm writing to be heard." This feeling of potentially being *heard* is a clear sign that the writer is maturing. The idea is not to shape what one says to an audience but to say it so that the audience understands the shape of what one says. This can be a very lonely experience at first. You are thinking on your own, unsure whether what you are saying will be received and understood. There is an element of risk to it that never goes away. It takes my students time to see one of the great paradoxes of writing; that it is a deeply personal act that can lead, at its best, to a very satisfying experience of a shared interpersonal reality. Even a private and very tentative thought can be shared with others, because after all, they too are full of private and very tentative thoughts. A common ground cleared for intelligent listening also helps prepare a student for work in the college classroom, where work also moves back and forth between many frames of reference.

~~~~~~~~~

I came to the idea of a narrative-based application as a tutor. I tried only to see what worked. I had no ideas or theories in mind. I started with students and whatever questions the colleges and universities were asking that year. Then I spent many hours trying to help them sort through their ideas before I saw I had to back up a little, helping them sort through the observations and feelings that led to those ideas. I have always been very struck by the *exactness* of the point of origin of those ideas. Often it was something they saw or something they felt about what they saw. Only rarely did they have an untraceable thought that occurred to them more or less out of nowhere. This may seem to be a limitation of the rational capacity of high school students, but in my work, I have come to think of it as a source of great strength. It gives their ideas, once they reach them, a pinpoint accuracy that is sometimes lacking in systems of highly elaborated abstractions. It also gives them well-defined check points to see, as clearly as possible, where they have been, where they are, and where they are going. The college application is a fertile field for drawing together this kind of large and grounded narrative, and the writing that results from an integrated process, such as the one I have tried to describe in this book, has a fullness of being that opens students to themselves, and to the world.

Conclusion

I WELL REMEMBER the moment when Harriet Sheridan, my English professor and then Dean of Carleton College, came up to me after I gave a short speech as part of a senior exercise. She was a magisterial woman with a head of white hair pulled back in a long, thick braid. I had spoken about the strange course of events by which the Roman Catholic Church had come to adopt celibacy as a rule in the tenth and eleventh centuries, not so much from any religious ideal but to keep the children of priests from inheriting Church property. "You have such a good sense of history," she told me. And it was true. Later at Harvard, I wrote two books about history and literature in the Victorian period. But at that moment, I still remember how vividly I felt *seen*.

It reminds me that a good part of tutorial is just this work of the student being seen by the tutor. I find I am often the first person to help them to begin to define who they are as thinkers and writers. This particular work of the tutor is sometimes misunderstood. I never give suggestions or guidance. I do not explain subjects systematically but introduce them selectively to see what takes hold. My aim is to provide a climate in which very little appears to come from me. Much does, of course, or else I could not have written this book. But again and again, my focus is always redirected to the student's internal experiencing of the world. The textual evidence of writing is what allows me access to this and what allows me to help refine it. For only in writing do students have hard evidence of an accepted inner referent, usually an experience they have recorded in deep and accurate detail. For once, their experience seems to have stabilized, if only provisionally, in prose. A text gives them a datum to return to for increasingly accurate directions that may emerge from it. Without this datum, I would be just another adjunct to their lives.

That said, I take care that the student relates to me only in and through writing. I am not a therapist. I avoid close relationships with my students and have them call me by my title, *Doctor*. What they take away from tutorial is not so much the sense of having worked with me—though that is certainly there—as the sense of having come into their own as writers. They first learn to own what they see and feel, becoming much less remote from their own experience. Then they learn to take responsibility for what they think about it by taking great care in expressing how they say what they say. As tutorial draws to a close, I begin to sense a receptiveness in the student. Usually when students come to me, they feel themselves to be experiencing an onslaught of knowledge that they are somehow *not* learning. When they leave, usually after a year or two of work, they share in common an ability to take pleasure in intellectual work. They also respond to what they read with a certain honest immediacy of response that translates well into writing. A great deal of movement has occurred, but much more is still to come. They are entering a world they never really knew existed. One in which the life of the mind no longer seems so strange to them, or even so very far.

Life always begins with chance. The people who raise you, the people they know, where you live, the schools you go to—none of these choices were made by *you*. You may or may not have access at first to the things that most deeply speak to you later on. The choice of a college is very often the first genuinely open choice a young person makes in our society. For once, the field is wide open. It is national, sometimes international. It crosses classes, religions, races, and cultures. Wherever you go, you are certain to find things you have never seen before. You may not be able to fit what you see to your preconceptions of it. Going to college involves an existential break. It involves a newness of perception, a discovery of the structure of an experience in the act of living it. Really living it, too, in the sense that family, religion, and neighborhood are all placed at one remove. The break also has an inward as well as an outward aspect. It involves changes in self-perception and in the perception of others. It entails being willing to release oneself to a certain sense of process, both objective and subjective, that has as its object not an end but an equilibrium, a state in which students have learned to establish a certain distance from things while, at the same time, beginning to be more confident in making their own observations about them.

Their *own*. Most of the indicators by which students are classed for consideration for college try to evaluate them by studying outcomes, not processes, and reducing these results to a few fixed numbers. This book has proposed a different measure. It looks at a student's writing as a representation of the process involved in intellectual change. If my students' essays have one thing in common, it is that they all begin the work of examining these changes in themselves. Our two essays again speak to this. The first, unrevised, presents a frozen moment. The second shows an ongoing moment, showing thought in its process of fermentation. This book has come to the conclusion that, in fostering intellectual change, what is needed first is to steep oneself in *events,* to approach what is seen with as few preconceptions as possible, taking a natural scientist's neutral, descriptive way of dealing with phenomena for which Darwin's *On the Origin of Species* is an enduring model, drawing limited inferences which seem most basic to the evidence itself. We have seen that a careful focus on writing tends to make students more sensitive to evidence embedded in events. My students learn that what they see and feel has to be cautiously explored before it can be named or labelled. They learn to be open to the unknown around them but on their own terms and in their own voice.

In this book, I have tried to describe the whole of the work of writing for admissions as it exists in the individual. I have found again and again that our best schools have responded openly to it. "They want what we want," I keep telling my students. "Don't think of them as different from me. They too look at you one at a time." I tell them as best I can that much of the work of admissions is always submerged in the writing of the student, and that the numbers represented by grades and scores are inherently misleading because they are lump sums. That it is in the exactness of writing that they can best present themselves. That any other measures are approximations in which they can scarcely hope to find themselves. That is why I have taken as my title a phrase that states this condition in two words: *admit one*.

It would be hoping for too much to expect that our system of admissions will change anytime soon. But, our way of preparing for admissions can. It can and should become more exploratory. In this book, I have tried out a way forward on a small scale. I hope I have shown that there are ways of working toward an admissions that can elicit the student without sacrificing rigor. Following several essays, we have seen that writing toward college admissions raises awareness to unexpected levels. For writing leads to a far different type of consciousness than that conditioned by grades and scores. A voice emerges. Again and again, I have seen that the degree of integration in a student's voice is a far more trustworthy measure of fitness for higher education than any set of numbers. The college admissions essay is, in many ways, an ideal field for seeing voice develop. Based on personal experience and making use of ideas, many often new to the student, it starts the student toward college with a life of the mind solidly established on a real base of conjoined seeing, feeling, and thinking. It does not take them out of social life by any means. Rather, it gives them an intellectual maturity, a sense of balance and distance, that allows them, once they reach college, to identify themselves, by their own choosing, with groups and institutions without losing any sense of their own inner identity. Seeing and feeling and thinking at last become *doing*. We could hardly ask for more.

INDEX

Thomas Richards has been an admissions consultant for ten years. He has an office in Haverford, Pennsylvania, and a website, admissionsreimagined.com. Richards was an associate professor of English and American literature at Harvard University. He has a PhD in English from Stanford University, an MA in English from the University of California, Berkeley, and a BA in English from Carleton College. He also has a BSc in geological sciences from the University of Hong Kong. He has written four other books: three works of literary and cultural criticism and one novel. They are *The Commodity Culture of Victorian England: Advertising and Spectacle, 1851–1914* (Stanford), *The Imperial Archive: Knowledge and the Fantasy of Empire* (Verso), *The Meaning of Star Trek* (Doubleday), and *Zero Tolerance* (Farrar, Straus & Giroux). He lives on Philadelphia's Main Line with his wife and two daughters.